Coming of Age

Identity Quests and the Adolescent Other in America's Television Culture

By
Jenn Burton

Leaning Rock Press
Gales Ferry, CT

Copyright © 2026, Jenn Burton

All rights reserved. No parts of this publication may be reproduced, stored in a database or retrieval system, or transmitted, in any form or by any means, without the prior permission of the author or publisher except by a reviewer who may quote brief passages in a review.

Leaning Rock Press
Gales Ferry, CT 06335
leaningrockpress@gmail.com
www.leaningrockpress.com

978-1-960596-88-8, Hardcover
978-1-960596-89-5, Softcover

Library of Congress Control Number: 2026901787

Publisher's Cataloging-in-Publication Data
(Prepared by Cassidy Cataloguing's PCIP Service)

Names:	Burton, Jenn, author.
Title:	Coming of age : identity quests and the adolescent other in America's television culture / by Jenn Burton.
Description:	Gales Ferry, CT : Leaning Rock Press, [2026] | Includes bibliographical references.
Identifiers:	LCCN: 2026901787 | ISBN: 9781960596888 (hardcover) | 9781960596895 (softcover)
Subjects:	LCSH: Television and teenagers. | Teenagers in mass media. | Teen television programs. | Teenagers--Psychology. | Identity (Psychology) | Self in adolescence. | Popular culture. | BISAC: SOCIAL SCIENCE / Anthropology / Cultural & Social. | SOCIAL SCIENCE / Media Studies. | SOCIAL SCIENCE / Popular Culture.
Classification:	LCC: HQ799.2.T4 B87 2026 | DDC: 302.23450835--dc23

Dedication

To Mom & Dad,

for their endless encouragement of my academic pursuits.

Table of Contents

Chapter 1 1

Theories on Television, Teenagers and Texts

Chapter 2 21

Vampires, Aliens & Messengers of God

Chapter 3 29

Buffy Summers as Set Apart

Chapter 4 35

Feeling Otherworldly in Roswell

Chapter 5 41

What Would Joan Do?

Chapter 6 47

Music & Money – Reaching the Teenagers

Chapter 7 63

This Is Who We Are: Central Characters as Surreal Teens

Chapter 8 93

Wait, Who Are We? Identity Quests of Buffy, Liz & Joan .

Chapter 9 121

Audience Responses

Chapter 10 147

Adolescents as the Real and Imagined “Chosen Ones”

About the author 150

Chapter 1

Theories on Television, Teenagers and Texts

The adolescent alienation from dominant culture is a subject that originally piqued my interest during my graduate program in American Studies. Through texts I was exposed to at the time, I realized that teens are an important subculture within America, not unlike women or middle-class workers or the Dust Bowl migrants of the early 20th century. There's a plethora of literature and analysis on these groups, so why isn't there more about this distinct subculture of teenagers often ignored by mainstream culture?

During the early 2000s, there were a few shows in particular that highlighted the teen character as alien or different from dominant culture. One of those shows was *Buffy the Vampire Slayer*, which premiered in 1997 and aired its last episode in 2003. *Buffy* competed with shows like *The O.C.*, *Dawson's Creek*, and earlier shows like *Beverly Hills, 90210*. On paper, the shows all fell within the "teen drama" category, but *Buffy* brought a new twist to the table, something we'd see in shows like *Roswell* and *Joan of Arcadia* during this time period as well. *Buffy the Vampire Slayer* was the show that started a genre of supernatural-based adolescent television shows: dramatic series for teen audiences that not only look at other worldly phenomena, but incorporate both spiritual and identity quests into their storylines. Buffy Summers was coming of age while she was also grappling with being the "Chosen One" of her generation, the slayer of all vampires (and evil). Her spiritual quest for fulfillment coincided with decisions about what prom dress to buy and which test to study for when she's strapped for time killing vampires in the graveyard.

Cultural analysts and sociologists have studied the effects of television on American culture for decades. But what has the impact been specifically on teenagers with messaging about spiritual and identity quests like the ones making a regular appearance in *Buffy's* storylines? According to JoEllen Fisherkeller in her work, *Growing Up with Television: Everyday Learning Among Young Adolescents*:

> The youth in this study, as a group of peers, understood that television is but one of many options people have for leisure, getting information, and interacting with others. And for them, TV was often the only option. Many of these adolescents regarded television as a necessary given, as shown in their disbelief when I informed them that I lived without cable TV (for a time). The idea that anyone did not have full access to television choices made some of their jaws drop.[1]

For teens of the early 2000s, television viewing was an extremely common activity, and teens chose shows for the ways in which their messages related to them individually. *Buffy the Vampire Slayer* deals with other-worldly forces, mostly because the main character, Buffy Summers, is the chosen one of her generation. She plays the role of the vampire slayer whom fate has selected to battle demons, vampires, and other creatures from hell. Being the "chosen one" means that Buffy has been pre-selected by destiny to fight evil. According to the vampire lore explained throughout the series, the history of the slayer dates back to prehistoric times. Buffy cannot resist her calling, because she is destined to fulfill this role.

One of the most engaging qualities exhibited by Buffy is her desire to be a "normal teenage girl". She has been given this immense responsibility to save the world (on multiple occasions), and what the viewer really sees throughout the series is Buffy's

1 JoEllen Fisherkeller, *Growing Up with Television: Everyday Learning Among Young Adolescents*. (Philadelphia: Temple University Press, 2002), 115.

own search for self. Her identity quest, and oftentimes, her spiritual awareness and discovery is a focal point of the show. And this would appeal to adolescents in so many different ways, as they are usually in a place in their own lives where they are trying to figure out who they are going to be, what and who they love, and how they are going to exist in this world. Buffy's relatability and her desire to fit in is an overarching theme of the show, and one that so many teens of the early 2000s could relate to.

Two years after *Buffy* originally aired, *Roswell* began airing on the WB network as well. Both *Roswell* and *Buffy* clearly dealt with supernatural forces. Three of *Roswell's* main characters are alien-human hybrids who are trying to live a normal teenage existence and also discover their identities as half-aliens. Both *Buffy's* and *Roswell's* lead characters engage in a search for self and, in so doing, begin the spiritual journeys which take place on these two television shows. The first episode of *Roswell* aired directly after *Dawson's Creek* on Wednesday, October 6, 1999 at 9:00pm on the WB network.[2] This time slot is important because the network (and writers of *Roswell*) were hoping to reach the same teen audience that tuned into *Dawson's Creek* each week. The first season of *Roswell* did not generate large numbers in the Nielsen ratings, with one example being the "Crazy" episode which came in at 1.9 (representing 1.9 million households viewing this episode). After season two did not bring many changes to the ratings, the series was dropped by WB network and picked up by UPN. Since the third season brought in similar ratings for the show as the first two seasons, *Roswell* was canceled in the spring of 2002.[3]

Although the ratings may not have been stellar for this series, *Roswell* fans gathered together on more than one occasion to save the show from cancellation prior to its third season. The storylines and characters presented on *Roswell* must have been something special in order for its viewers to send an unusual present to UPN after the WB dropped the show. "*Buffy's* new home, UPN was bombarded this week with thousands of bottles of Tabasco Sauce, sent

2 *Roswell* on TV.com. CNET Networks, Inc. Updated 2006, www.tv.com

3 "News for *Roswell*." Internet Movie Database Inc. Updated 2006. www.imdb.com

by dedicated *Roswell* fans. The campaign slogan: Spice Up Your Lineup – Add *Roswell* to UPN!"[4] Unfortunately for these avid fans, their efforts only bought the show one more season on the air. However, of most significance here is the fact that both *Buffy* and *Roswell* were first on the WB network, very shortly after the creation of this network by founder and CEO Jamie Kellner in 1995. According to the Encyclopedia of Television, "it was the Fox-produced *Buffy the Vampire Slayer* that truly sparked the network's success streak and established the teen audience the network craved."[5] Thus, *Buffy* and *Roswell* were largely responsible for the popularity of the WB network among its teen audience.

The third show under analysis here takes a slightly different approach to dealing with adolescent alienation and teen identity quests. *Joan of Arcadia* began airing on the CBS network in 2003, and was canceled after just two seasons. This show was built on the premise that God speaks to an adolescent female, Joan, through individuals in her everyday life. The main storylines in this show are founded on issues of adolescent identity, questioning of the spiritual world, and the relationship between human existence and the supernatural. The first episode of *Joan of Arcadia* premiered on September 26, 2003 and the series finale aired on April 22, 2005. According to an article from *The Associated Press*, "During its first season, *Joan of Arcadia* averaged 10.1 million viewers, respectable numbers for Friday, a quiet night for television. This year, viewership sank to 8 million, according to Nielsen Media Research."[6] Just as *Roswell* was canceled due to low ratings, *Joan of Arcadia* was replaced on CBS and the genre of supernatural teen television dramas lost another show representing the teen alienation and identity quests that set *Buffy*, *Roswell*, and *Joan of Arcadia* apart from other teen dramas.

4 "About, Inc." The New York Times Company. Updated 2006. http://history1900s.about.com

5 Routledge, Taylor & Francis Group. "Encyclopedia of Television". Updated by Routledge in 2004. www.routledge-ny.com/ref/television/wbnet.html.

6 "Fans demand Joan, fight CBS over cancellation." The Associated Press, May 30, 2005. www.tv.com

Coming of Age

The focal series in this study all initially aired at the crossroads of the 20th and 21st centuries. During this time, the supernatural elements of *Buffy*, *Roswell*, and *Joan of Arcadia* were generally accepted among the teen audience, as seen in the audience response to these series. The continuing supernatural programming as seen in television programs such as *Supernatural* and *Heroes*, provide evidence to the adult assumption of ongoing interest among teens and young adult viewers in supernatural television dramas.

It's important to keep in mind the conceptual considerations of the adult construction of adolescent reality, the introduction of media representations of teens as alien others in dominant culture in the early 2000s, and the role of television shows and social media in the lives of real teens across more than two decades. What is being said (or unsaid) about the supernatural "other" among adolescents in *Buffy the Vampire Slayer* that we see repeated in mainstream culture twenty years later? What is the significance of the spiritual and identity quest in the early 2000s as opposed to the presentation of self to others through the social media lens of post-pandemic 2020s? Television was a shaping force in American culture from its birth in the 1950s, and more than seventy years later, television is still a shaping force, along with the new force of social media driving cultural trends, popularity, and even celebrity status.

In attempting to answer these cultural questions, it is a fundamental assertion throughout this study that television has been (and continues to be) a shaping force for adolescents in post-World War II America. The power of media in American culture, coupled with the importance of examining adolescence within this culture offers a broad foundation for analysis into constructions of adolescence by the adults who write and produce these shows, and the reality that real teens embrace, reproduce, or reject. Accordingly, in an attempt to further understand and appreciate the position of adolescents in American culture, it is crucial to analyze the representation of teen life as outside the adult norm through the visual imagery presented by *Buffy*, *Roswell*, and *Joan of Arcadia*. On a deeper level, the appeal of and the meanings behind this representation of adolescents must be uncovered in order to both recognize teens as a significant cultural group and to understand adolescent culture as an important part of American culture.

In this intensive study of three television shows, it is important to outline the key theoretical terms that will be used throughout this research endeavor. First, "real teens" refers to the actual adolescents living in America during the study period. These are the individuals who are not yet fully enculturated into nor completely validated members of mainstream culture, and who are arguably affected by the media representations of teens presented by these particular shows. Real teens are not to be confused with the characters on these television shows, although there are characteristics that will be identified as shared by both the teen characters and the real teens to be discussed in this study.

The second major term to outline is the adolescent construction of reality.[7] I use the term "adolescent construction of reality" to explain the way in which teens develop a belief system and a mental picture of real life. It is my claim that television shows such as *Buffy the Vampire Slayer*, *Roswell*, and *Joan of Arcadia*, while in fact the creations or constructions of adults, are valued by real teens and hence act as catalysts in the adolescent construction of reality.

The final phrase that must be explained in detail is the concept of "not belonging" in American society. This phrase will be utilized to describe the experiences of alienated cultural groups that are set apart from mainstream culture because dominant ideology does not allow room for the beliefs and practices of these groups to be included in the mainstream collective memory. For example, many teens struggle with fitting in with the popular crowd in high school. Their search for belonging occurs within their subculture of adolescents, as well as within the dominant culture. Teens must accept some of the values of mainstream culture in order to survive in America, but this does not mean that teens are accepted members

7 This is a term that I adopted from a course taught by Dr. Pamela Steinle in Fall 2004 semester at California State University, Fullerton, titled "Adolescent America," in which major themes of teen culture were explored.

of the dominant culture. In many ways, teens have been outsiders since the recognition of this distinct and liminal social category in the 1940s. Liminal in this case refers to the in-between life stage of adolescents, in which one is no longer a child but is not considered an adult either.

In order to examine adolescent culture in America, it is crucial to outline the meaning of culture within this study. In this cultural analysis, the culture concept theory provided by Clifford Geertz lays the foundation.

> The culture concept to which I adhere has neither multiple referents nor, so far as I can see, any unusual ambiguity: it denotes an historically transmitted pattern of meanings embodied in symbols, a system of inherited conceptions expressed in symbolic forms by means of which men communicate, perpetuate, and develop their knowledge about and attitudes toward life.[8]

Geertz's culture concept is based on the belief that a culture is defined by its symbols, and that these symbols carry meaning for that particular cultural group. Along with this framework, Geertz offers significant symbols that give meaning to cultural events. Television is a significant medium of symbol production in American culture, and this is especially true in the world of adolescents. Television has changed the everyday lives of post-World War II Americans, and provided them with a modern source of both news and entertainment. The TV set became the center of the family home in the 1950s, and more than seventy years later, critics argue that television, technology, cell phones and social media have torn the family apart. Instead of talking to one another, each member of the family unit retreats to his or her respective television or cell phone or laptop computer. For these reasons, television claimed a distinct and meaningful role in society as a producer of not only symbols but also viewing groups or subcultures in American culture. In this study of the relationship between the lives of real teens and the televisual texts of teen drama series, the culture concept provided

8 Clifford Geertz, *The Interpretation of Cultures*. (New York: Basic Books, 1973), 89.

by Geertz recognizes the importance of cultural symbols and the producers of those cultural symbols.

In further understanding this relationship between teenagers and television, an understanding of the history of American adolescence and its connection to the lives of real teens through the representations of teens on television shows must be developed. As television emerged in the same post-World War II context, simultaneous with the expansion of teen culture, it is crucial to take a step back and look at the impact of television on American culture. As media and social historian Lynn Spigel argues in *Make Room for TV*, "the television set became an integral part of the domestic environment" of post-World War II culture.[9] Spigel explains that TV culture was and is a distinctly American feature, shaped by the societal conditions at the time of the emergence of television as an everyday part of life. In post-World War II American culture, the family ideal and the beliefs regarding domesticity began to shift in a movement back to the home for American women. The television set became an important part of family life, as its presence became more and more prominent in homes across the country. As Spigel describes the support and warnings given by the public,

> Utopian statements that idealized the new medium as an ultimate expression of technological and social progress were met by equally dystopian discourses that warned of television's devastating effects on family relationships and the efficient functioning of the household. Television was not simply promoted; rather, it was something that had to be questioned and deliberated upon.[10]

The impact of television on American culture is a much-discussed topic amongst sociologists and cultural analysts. The historical impact of American culture lends a unique understanding to the intensity of the impact on adolescents specifically at the turn of the 21st century. Cecilia Tichi, an English professor at Vanderbilt University, has also examined the emergence of television as

9 Lynn Spigel, *Make Room for TV: Television and the Family Ideal in Postwar America*. (Illinois: University of Chicago Press, 1992), 37.

10 Spigel, 3.

a cultural force, but she only extends her analysis to the late 20th century. In her book, *Electronic Hearth*, Tichi explores the many ways in which television has infiltrated American culture, especially before the social media explosion of more recent years. Writing in 1991, Tichi claims that "television is by now ubiquitous in virtually every cultural format and venue in the United States. It takes shape as familial hearth, as the illuminator/corruptor of children, as the paradoxical site of sedentary activism, as the locus of a new, multivalent consciousness."[11] Tichi explores the cultural image of the television as the new family center, replacing the fireplace in American homes, and essentially changing the way families interact with each other at home. Her book also focuses on the ways in which television takes over leisure hours for children and adults alike. The leisure culture that began to emerge in America in the 1950s changed the way many Americans lived in their time outside of work, and watching television became one of the most prevalent ways to spend leisure time. Similar to social media's impact of the 2020s, the television set acts as a companion for many Americans, including adolescents, and television became more privatized in the last quarter of the 20th century. Like Spigel, Tichi examines the impact of television on American culture, as well as the impact on the family unit and the individuals within the family.

A specific genre of programming for adolescents began to develop late in the 20th century. In his book, *Gen X TV*, television critic Rob Owen provides a broad overview of shows from the 1980s and 1990s, their impact on familial relationships in America and, specifically, those that fundamentally shaped the development of Generation X. At the heart of Owen's argument lies the contention that the children who were raised on TV and grew up with the strong presence of consumer culture in the 1980s and 1990s have made a significant impact on the power of television shows. The changes within the American family have caused television to be even more important in the lives of American adolescents. Owen views the relationship between television and adolescents

---

11 Cecilia Tichi. *Electronic Hearth: Creating an American Television Culture.* (New York: Oxford University Press, 1991), 209.

(specifically Generation X teens) as reciprocal, with each influencing the other. He writes:

> Although not the first group of Americans to grow up on TV, Xers are the first group for whom TV served as a regularly scheduled baby-sitter. Gen X was the first to experience MTV and the FOX network, and they are an audience many advertisers are eager to reach. Xers are the most media-savvy generation ever.[12]

The Gen X teens are different because they are more likely to be the children of divorced and blended families than previous generations which, Owen argues, means they adopt TV families such as *The Brady Bunch* as their own family. Many teens admired but could not actually relate to characters on shows like *Beverly Hills, 90210* during the 1990s. Along came shows like *Buffy* that spoke to a new audience of teenagers about not belonging, and wanting to be something more, and that spoke to a lot of adolescents in the late 20th century. They wanted an unlikely hero, someone like them, but also someone with a uniqueness that was unparalleled.

Essentially, Spigel, Tichi, and Owen all focus on the relationship between individuals and television in the last half of the 20th century. They examine the role of television in the changing nature of family relationships, which was directly seen in the world of adolescents as their cultural role and position shifted and teens became a subculture rather than simply members of a certain life stage. Spigel and Tichi provide historical information regarding the development of television culture and the impact of leisure time on the prominence of television in the lives of Americans. Owen continues with the theme of familial relationships and the ways in which families were impacted by the television set. However, he carries it into a later time period and uses specific television shows to discuss these cultural changes. These studies provide a cultural foundation for a more narrowly defined look at the teen television genre that includes *Buffy*, *Roswell*, and *Joan of Arcadia*. In my analysis

12 Rob Owens. Gen X TV: *The Brady Bunch to Melrose Place.* (New York: Syracuse University Press, 1997), 5.

of episodes and teen characters, I use the historical work of Spigel, Tichi and Owen to determine what sets these new teen television dramas apart from earlier shows and how the subculture of teens has been affected by this new style of teen dramas.

Along with the identification of television as a noteworthy force in American culture, it is important to discuss the term "cultural image" as presented by Susan Bordo in her analysis of visual images in America. In *Twilight Zones: The Hidden Life of Cultural Images From Plato to O.J.*, Bordo contends that cultural images are visual texts within societies, such as television, print ads, and movies, which carry specific connotations. The media are hugely responsible for the cultural images that are presented to the American public. Bordo argues that it is the duty of cultural analysts to deeply consider these images and their meanings.

> It is essential that we cultivate the practice of turning a critical light on popular culture, particularly among our children and students, who were born into this world of created images and are an important target of its seductions.[13]

These visual images, including the media representations of teens in television shows, are significant symbols within American culture. Bordo's argument encourages a close look at the various elements of *Buffy*, *Roswell*, and *Joan of Arcadia* as cultural images that must be critically analyzed.

In terms of the reception of images, literary theorist Stanley Fish presents a theory based on the influence of interpretive communities in understanding, or reading, a text. In analyzing themes in *Buffy the Vampire Slayer*, *Roswell*, and *Joan of Arcadia*, interpreting visual texts is a necessary step. A text is basically any cultural document, including written text in books, articles, poetry, and song lyrics, as well as visual texts such as film, television, art, and photography. In the case of this research, the interpretive community of adolescents (which can be further broken down to split adolescents into distinct groups based on gender, class, race or ethnicity) reads

13 Susan Bordo, *Twilight Zones: The Hidden Life of Cultural Images From Plato to O.J.* (California: University of California Press, 1999). 14-15.

television texts in a different manner than their adult counterparts. For instance, a middle-aged man watching an episode of *Buffy the Vampire Slayer* may identify with different characters, storylines, and language – and likely generate different meanings – than an adolescent female watching the same show. Fish argues that, "it is interpretive communities, rather than either the text or the reader, that produce meanings and are responsible for the emergence of formal features."[14] Unlike many literary theorists, Stanley Fish allows the viewer's interpretive community to play a role in the understanding of a given cultural text.

Commercial culture and the expansion of product placement in the already teenage-saturated world of television also influenced the content of *Buffy*, *Roswell*, and *Joan of Arcadia*. During the original airing of these shows beginning with *Buffy* in 1997 and ending with *Joan of Arcadia* in 2005, many consumer items and advertisements were presented to the viewer, both during commercial breaks and on the shows themselves by way of product placement. Although this study does not focus on the effect of advertising and the relationship between consumer culture and adolescents, it is important to recognize that product placement on these television series as well as the commercials shown throughout the original airing of each both played a role in furthering the impact of these television series among teenagers by integrating their viewing experience with the realm of everyday activities in consumer culture.

Product placement and pop culture references on television shows have an impact on the viewer, whether that viewer is able to recognize it or not at the time. According to journalist Alissa Quart in *Branded: The Buying and Selling of Teenagers*, "...the placement of products is not just visual in the new teen fare. The films [and television series] celebrate brands in their dialogue."[15] Indeed, this integration of consumer products within popular cultural expression is startingly seamless in television programming for adolescents. *Buffy*

14 Stanley Fish. *Is There a Text In This Class? The Authority of Interpretive Communities*. (Massachusetts: Harvard University Press, 1980), 14.

15 Alissa Quart. *Branded: The Buying and Selling of Teenagers*. (Massachusetts: Perseus Publishing, 2003), 90.

is notorious for its pop culture references, from the first episode with Xander referring to Sunnydale as "a one-Starbucks town" to Buffy's complaint of itchy skin after being infected by a demon: "Anyway, it's been itching like crazy. No big. Just another problem for the good people at Lubriderm, right?"[16] Product placement and pop culture references are also evident in *Roswell*. Consider, for instance, an episode entitled "Tess, Lies and Videotape" as an obvious reference to the 1989 film *Sex, Lies and Videotape* – or a third season episode in which Michael is accused of stealing a case of Snapple at work. *Joan of Arcadia* also contains both pop culture references and product placement. In an early episode, for instance, when Joan observes that she is having a bad hair day, she complains to her mom that she looks "like Coolio": a rapper from the 1990s. Thus, even though viewers may or may not consciously recognize the product placement and pop culture references, the presence of these advertising tools of American consumerism is undeniable in these shows.

The final major theory that I am working with throughout this research comes from Avery Gordon's work in *Ghostly Matters: Haunting and the Sociological Imagination*. Ghostly subjects in American experience are those events that cause cultural change or trauma resulting in unresolved issues or questions and, hence, continue to haunt our culture. In many cases, the "ghostly matter" is the sign that an issue has not been fully dealt with in the American experience. In studying adolescent culture, it has become evident that many adolescents – and adolescent expressive forms – experience and/or express alienation from the dominant culture as it evades confrontation with the issues that face teens in America today, creating ghostly matters. Gordon writes, "Haunting is an encounter in which you touch the ghost or the ghostly matter of things: the ambiguities, the complexities of power and personhood, the violence and the hope, the looming and receding actualities, the shadows of our selves and our society."[17] A ghostly matter allows individuals to reflect on a

16 *Buffy the Vampire Slayer*, Season 3, Episode 18.

17 Avery Gordon. *Ghostly Matters: Haunting and the Sociological Imagination*. (Minnesota: University of Minnesota Press, 1997), 134.

certain event, person, or cultural group because it brings the issue to light. That reflection is a necessary part of the present and does not simply exist in retrospect. If the ghostly matter in society can be recognized in the present, maybe it can be dealt with and not just ignored until it tears apart society. Through an analysis of teen television programs that focus on the teen as an outsider to dominant culture, this research will incorporate the ideas of Gordon in determining how the culture must reckon with its ghosts.

Gordon's theory has been one of the most influential in this study, as it provides a foundation for looking at cultural groups or events that have been ignored by mainstream culture. Teens in America are often not taken seriously, because they are not always recognized as individuals who are part of the dominant culture. In reckoning with cultural ghosts, Gordon suggests that issues that have previously been overlooked by mainstream American culture must be confronted head-on. Therefore, in applying Gordon's theory to this study on adolescent culture and television series that represent the alienation of teens by dominant culture, I am using Gordon's broad cultural argument of ghostly matters in American culture to explore the lives of real teens living as members of the subculture of adolescents coping with issues of not belonging.

The cultural theories provided by Geertz, Fish, and Gordon lay the cultural and historical foundation before turning to a more specialized analysis of the subculture of teens and their relationship to the media. As teenagers become more and more marginalized, and labeled as an outsider, their quest for something meaningful deepens. Teenagers in American culture are often not taken seriously, because they are not always recognized as individuals who are part of the dominant culture. Thus, teenagers exist on the outskirts, in their own subculture within dominant culture. They walk a thin line of belonging and being ostracized, of being taken seriously and written off as meaningless or unimportant. As Lynn Schofield Clark discusses in her book, *From Angels to Aliens*, the lives of teenagers are forever changing and teens are constantly seeking: "Certainly, the teenage years are a time of confusion, as significant physical, emotional, social and sometimes even spiritual changes define the period that marks the transition from childhood to adulthood."[18] As teens search for what they believe, they often engage in a type of spiritual quest. This search for meaning and purpose in a larger context than their everyday lives can often take on the form of religious experimentation for teens or identification with a certain belief system.

In her larger overarching argument, Clark contends that the questions many teens face during these formative years are not confronted or taken seriously by adults in the dominant societal group, and this has created quite an identity crisis for America's adolescents. A phenomenon that we see continuing in the 2020s, as social media encourages teenagers to be themselves, but then rates videos and compares them to one another based on likes and shares. It is my argument that tragic events during the turn of the 21st century (the Columbine High School shooting in 1999 and the terrorist attacks of September 11, 2001) ignited and intensified this identity crisis for teens once again.

In her study, Clark questioned many real teens about their response to supernatural television shows, and then looked at their responses in terms of their religious traditions. Her conclusion suggests that teens are able to make the distinction between fantasy in the media and reality of life as a teenager in America. Clark also examines *Buffy the Vampire Slayer* in detail, along with other supernatural shows such as *Charmed* and *Buffy's* spin-off series, *Angel.* Her argument regarding the spiritual questing of teens provides a foundation for analyzing the importance and influence of supernatural elements in teen TV.

Adolescence, as defined by developmental psychologists, is a universal life stage that is biologically driven and also reflects sociological imperatives. Virtually ignored in the seventeenth and eighteenth centuries, American adolescence has been described as a tumultuous and defining period of time in an individual's life since the nineteenth century. Thomas Hine, author of *The Rise and Fall*

---

18 Lynn Schofield Clark. *From Angels to Aliens: Teenagers, the Media, and the Supernatural.* (New York: Oxford University Press, 2003), 4.

of the American Teenager, examines the social category of the teenager as it emerged in the twentieth century as an expression of adolescent participation in American life. For Hine, teenagers are neither adults nor children, and they are constantly in a state of limbo in American culture. Hine also suggests that the idea of the American teenager does not need to continue in our society, due in large part to its negative connotations, which have developed in reference to teenagers over time.

According to Hine, "teenagers occupy a special place in the society. They are envied and sold to, studied and deplored. They are expected to break some rules, but there are other restrictions that apply only to them. They are at a golden moment in life – and not to be trusted."[19] As a result of this stereotypical notion of the teenager, there is a huge gap of information between what Americans believe about "teens" versus the reality of the individual experiences of teenagers. Also, each new generation of teenagers is constantly changing, which poses a problem for the mainstream society that fears deviant behavior and is uneasy about the youth culture at large. Interestingly, this fearful group of adults in mainstream society is composed of former teens. According to Hine, this teenage mystique, then, simply serves to perpetuate a false perception of what it means to be a teenager in America, because society has chosen to ignore the voices of the real teens.

So what led to the defining of an entire subgroup of people in American culture? Hine points to the "emergence of high school as a common experience of young Americans [which] led directly to the emergence of teenagers as we know them today."[20] In fact, Hine states that in American society, "to reject high school is to reject the society as a whole."[21] High school became a common obstacle that all teenagers shared. Hine claims that society insists on this shared experience, and anyone who does not attend high school or drops out before graduation is labeled as a deviant. Yet,

---

19 Thomas Hine. *The Rise and Fall of the American Teenager*. (New York, Avon Books, Inc., 1999), 10.

20 Hine, 204.

21 Hine, 139.

according to Hine, high school is an institution that has lost its sense of direction, or has been given too many tasks to differentiate what is actually important for the teenager to learn during these critical years. Hine argues that the contemporary high school basically serves as a holding place for teenagers, because society has no specific place for them. I agree with much of what Hine is arguing here, in that high school has become a place where teenagers are taught little or no life skills to help them survive outside of public school institutions. Many high school students who are unsuccessful in this regimented system lead extremely productive lives once they leave the peer pressure and standardized testing behind.

It is crucial to remember that the teens of the 1950s were unlike the teenagers of the 1970s, and both were markedly different from the teens of the 1990s. Fast forward another thirty years, and the teenagers of the 2020s are an entirely different animal. Hine, in the late 1990s, argued that the idea of the teenager does not need to be a part of the future, but if it is, we need to re-shape the teenage experience into a rewarding one. He states that teenagers are beginners who need help as they embark on the journey to adulthood. Teenagers should be encouraged to experiment with different life paths, and not stereotyped because of their individual choices. Patricia Hersch echoes Hine's sentiments in her study of contemporary adolescence, *A Tribe Apart*, published in 1998. Hersch writes, "Adolescence is a journey, a search for self in every dimension of being. It is about dreams, fears, and hopes, as much as about hormones, SAT scores, and fashion. It is about endless possibilities as well as dead ends."[22] Thus, the journey of adolescence leads down a challenging and often confusing path for many American teenagers – and no less so for their fictive counterparts on shows of the late 1990s like *Buffy the Vampire Slayer*. Take this a step farther into the 2020s, and the confusing paths have become more varied, as identity quests now include not only what the teenager wants to do with the rest of their lives, or what values they hold dear, but also gender identity and fluidity with categories that used to be fixed in our society.

---

22 Patricia Hersch. *A Tribe Apart: A Journey Into the Heart of American Adolescence.* (New York: Random House Inc., 1998), 17.

In this study, episodes from the television series noted herein will be analyzed. Because of the distinctly teenage focus of this study, seasons one through three of *Buffy*, seasons one through three of *Roswell*, and season one of *Joan of Arcadia* will be focused on. Along with an in-depth analysis of the major themes and issues in these episodes, I conducted interviews and examined responses on fan websites, online reviews, and other Internet sources available in the early 2000s. Just as Stanley Fish argues for the importance of an interpretive community to provide their understanding of a certain cultural text, I use audience responses and interpretations as a representative reading of teen television shows by the interpretive community of adolescents.

In the televisual world of teen dramas that focus solely on the normative aspects of teen life, supernatural teen series speak to the alienation of real teens in America today. In the chapters to come, I argue that *Buffy*, *Roswell*, and *Joan of Arcadia* are fictive representations of the outsider status of real teens, as evidenced by the characterizations, supernatural identity quests, and major themes of each of these television series. The response of real teens to these supernatural teen dramas tells a story of real life teen angst highlighted by supernatural elements on these three television shows.

I begin with overviews of each show in chapter two, including character information, major themes and storylines, and music – both in theme songs and music featured in each program. Chapters three, four and five focus on main characters of these teen series as set apart, even withing the subculture of teens. In chapter six, I explore the way in which main characters on each show are represented as "hyper-real teens." By this, I mean that these characters are fictional, yet they act as illustrations of real teens in American culture. They are symbols of the type of real teens that the show's writers are trying to bring to the television screen. Chapter seven focuses on the normative qualities of teen culture and the ways in which the teen character on *Buffy*, *Roswell*, and *Joan of Arcadia* represent these normative qualities.

Chapter eight examines the identity quests of the main characters of each show. The spiritual and other-worldly roles that Buffy,

Liz, and Joan play are connected to larger questions of spirituality, otherness, and being chosen. I will explore how these characters represent feminism and autonomy in their authenticity and continuous search for meaning. Chapter nine will analyze audience responses to these three shows, and link the world of television characters to real teens. Finally, chapter ten will focus on the ways in which adolescents are represented as the chosen ones, both in reality and in these television programs. This chapter will explore the ways in which these shows interact with teens in real life, and the effect that they have on American adolescent culture and its participants. By exploring the characters of these three shows as outsiders on a spiritual quest, this analysis will attempt to identify and solve for the absence of the supernatural other in shows in post-pandemic America in the 2020s.

Chapter 2

Vampires, Aliens & Messengers of God

"I never knew being a teenager was so full of possibilities."[23] In the sarcastic words of Buffy Summers, it is clear throughout *Buffy the Vampire Slayer* that the lives of teenagers are anything but easy. In the case of Buffy Summers, teenage existence is terrifying, unpredictable, and often messy. The heroine of this series is constantly portrayed as being alone, the "Chosen One" selected by fate to fight demons, vampires, and other evil creatures. She has a support system in her mother, friends, and her watcher (the vampire slayer's mentor), but at the end of the day, she's usually fighting alone. Although Buffy may be at times resistant to her calling as the slayer, she ultimately knows that she must be independent and capable of fighting to save the world. She must be willing to sacrifice her own life to protect the lives of everyone around her.

Buffy the Vampire Slayer (also referred to simply as *Buffy* herein) began airing on the WB network in 1997 and is often credited with the early success of this network. The main character, Buffy Summers, is "the Chosen One", as explained in the opening credits of the first season. "In every generation, there is a Chosen One. She alone will stand against the vampires, the demons, and the forces of darkness. She is the Slayer."[24] These words locate the viewer in presupposed context of conflict between good and evil, as well as identifying Buffy as someone special, someone who has been selected to do the work of slaying evil that many people could not do.

23 *Buffy the Vampire Slayer*, Season 1, Episode 5.

24 *Buffy the Vampire Slayer*, Season 1 , Episode 11.

As the Chosen One, Buffy is the lead character of this television series, but she does not work in complete isolation from her surroundings or her peers. Buffy exists in two worlds: the teen culture/high school community and the slayer culture/vampire community. Central characters such as Buffy's best friends, Willow and Xander, as well as her watcher, Mr. Giles, join her in both of these worlds as she lets them in on her secret destiny and role. The adolescent characters (Buffy's friends and enemies in the high school community) are arguably much like any other teen character on shows of that era such as *The O.C.* or *One Tree Hill.* They are even like today's social media influencers in many ways. Most of these teens (past and present) gossip with their friends, argue with their parents, and often believe that insignificant details are life-altering circumstances. The supernatural elements of this show, however, set *Buffy* apart in ways that are not seen in many other teen shows. The presence of a strong female is not a common trait on television shows at the turn of the 21st century, and the fact that Buffy is the Chosen One complicates her love life, academic performance, and familial relationships in different ways. The characters on this show complement the major theme that Buffy has a destiny, a calling in life beyond boys, school and cheerleading.

Similarly on *Roswell*, Max is distinctly set apart from the "in crowd" and is viewed by many of his peers as an odd guy. The audience soon learns that Max has a secret: he is actually half-alien, created by the inhabitants of his home planet by mixing alien genetic material with human DNA to create a unique genetic composition. Max's interactions with Liz Parker soon lead him to let her in on the secret – making her chosen by the supernatural in a way that parallels Buffy's selection as the chosen one. In *Roswell*, one major storyline is the love story between Max and Liz, which bridges the gap between humans and alien hybrids even further.

On *Joan of Arcadia*, the dominant storyline is around Joan's ability to carry out God's will as a teenage girl. Joan is chosen by God even though she has a somewhat shaky past with religion, including promises to God that she would be a better person if he allowed her older brother, Kevin, to live after a horrific car accident. Joan struggles in the first season of the show to come to terms with why she has been chosen by God, but even as she does not fully understand it, she tries to fulfill the duties asked of her. Joan's role as an adolescent, and a female adolescent in particular, makes her an unlikely candidate to act as a messenger of God. Joan is often uneasy about being chosen by God, and her spiritual quest is complicated by her own doubts about God's existence.

All three shows are centered on high school life as is typical of other dramatic teen television series. This reinforces the idea that high school is the center of teen culture. Another common trait of teen dramas including *Buffy*, *Roswell*, and *Joan of Arcadia* is the use of powerful theme songs. The lyrics of each theme song are extremely powerful, providing a literal framing of the series emphasis. The common setting of high school, as well as the shared themes of friendship, romance, and family struggles link these series with other teen dramas such as *Dawson's Creek*, which aired in the same time period as *Buffy* and *Roswell.* However, it is the spiritual questing and confrontation with "evil" that highlights the "otherness" of teen experience in these shows.

The adolescent characters on *Buffy*, *Roswell* and *Joan of Arcadia* are arguably much like any other teen character that you may find on *The O.C.* or *Dawson's Creek* or *One Tree Hill* which aired during the same time period as the three shows being analyzed in this study. The supernatural elements of these shows set the main characters apart in ways that are not seen in other television shows of that time period. The characters on *Buffy*, for instance, complement the major theme that Buffy has a destiny – she has been called to do something more than fall in love, go to school, and be a cheerleader. But that does not mean that Buffy does not still want those typical teenage experiences.

As the third season of *Buffy* came to a close, two new series began on the WB the following fall: *Dawson's Creek* and *Roswell.* *Dawson's Creek* centered on the lives of high school teens in small-town Capeside, Massachusetts. *Dawson's Creek* and *Roswell* both aimed to appeal to the teen audience that *Buffy* had brought to the WB network.

> WB executives gloated that *Dawson's Creek* had been rejected by Fox before finding its way to the network. As the

> Fox network abandoned its initial youthful identity in an attempt to "age" their network with programs like *Ally McBeal*, the WB became the number one network among teens in the U.S. just three years after its launch, enjoying a 32% increase in ratings among teens 12 to 17 that season.[25]

The teen angst on *Dawson's Creek* was centered on issues faced by "normal" white, middle-class to working-class teens such as struggles with sexual intimacy, being the children of divorced parents, and feeling betrayed by a best friend. By contrast, *Roswell* picked up on some of the supernatural themes that *Buffy* had just confronted. Buffy went off to college where she continued to fight evil, and the teen viewers of this network were introduced to a new high school cast set in the town of Roswell, New Mexico. The show's summary from TV.com reads: "*Roswell* is about teenage alien-human hybrids living in Roswell, New Mexico who attempted to survive as humans and hide their alien sides, while trying to learn more about their alien powers, as well as figuring out how to get home."[26]

This brief synopsis does not even begin to delve into the characters, major themes, and teen issues that were presented on *Roswell* weekly. The major themes of *Roswell* resembled those of *Buffy*, while also exploring the "normal" issues of teen angst presented by the more traditional teen dramas on air at the time. The themes of *Roswell* combined the supernatural elements with the everyday issues, resulting in a range of topics from teen romance to conflicts between parents and teens, teen friendships, and questioning one's identity and role in the world. The major characters include three extraterrestrial alien-human hybrids: Max Evans, his sister Isabel, and their friend Michael Guerin. The other central characters are humans who learn the secret identity of Max, Isabel and Michael throughout the series. The most significant of these human characters is Liz Parker, Max's romantic interest and a bridge between human and alien in more ways than one.

---

25 The Museum of Broadcast Communications Encyclopedia of Television. "WB Network." Routledge 2004. www.routledge-ny.com

26 TV.com. *Roswell.* TV Show. Copyright 2006 by CNET Networks, Inc. www.tv.com

Max Evans is the alien-human hybrid who falls in love with human Liz Parker and heals her when she is shot at the CrashDown Café where she works. Healing is Max's alien power: he cures the wounds of humans when the death is unnecessary or caused by a spontaneous violent act. We see this again in the show when Max heals Kyle, then a group of children in the hospital, and Liz again when she is suffering from an alien-induced virus later on in the show. Max also acts as the contemplative moral guide and leader of this group of friends. Viewers learn that Max was actually the king on his home planet, which explains his natural leadership qualities in *Roswell.*

Max's sister, Isabel, is also an alien-human hybrid. As very young children, Isabel, Max and Michael came out of the alien pods that were sent to Earth and crashed in Roswell. Upon exiting the pods, Max and Isabel immediately knew they had a sibling connection, whereas Michael was apparently unrelated. After wandering in the desert, Isabel, Max and Michael made their way into the town and are believed to be orphans abandoned by their human parents. Isabel and Max are adopted and Michael is placed in foster care.

Michael's foster father only keeps him around for the government checks he receives, while Max and Isabel's parents are loving and present. Michael is rebellious, closed-off emotionally, and in desperate search of his alien roots in order to find his place in the world. Michael is extremely abrasive and selfish for much of the series, but the audience is able to see a softer side of Michael when he becomes involved in a romantic relationship with Maria DeLuca, Liz Parker's best friend.

Liz Parker is the main female character on *Roswell,* and she is romantically linked to Max Evans. Liz is a small-town girl who works at the alien-inspired CrashDown Café owned by her parents. Liz is well-liked, and a good student. In the first episode of the series, Liz is the victim of a gunshot wound as the result of a conflict between two customers in the café. Max is there and intercedes to save Liz, removing the bullet from her body and healing her.

In many ways, *Joan of Arcadia* is a much different show than *Buffy* and *Roswell.* First, it airs on a completely different network and is presented as a family show. *Joan* began airing on CBS network in September 2003. It ran for two seasons and was then canceled. Interestingly enough, *Joan of Arcadia* is classified as a drama according to TV.com, while both *Buffy* and *Roswell* are classified as sci-fi adventure dramas. Apparently, this is a reflection of the distinction between secular (sci-fi) and Biblical (Christian) supernatural themes for studios and television producers in the early 21st century. The supernatural elements in *Joan of Arcadia* revolve around her conversations with God, and the messages that Joan receives from God to carry out his will on Earth. Yet, the focus of this show is often perceived to be the family and, in particular, the relationship between a teenage girl and her family as the synopsis from TV.com states. "*Joan of Arcadia* is a drama that follows a typical family facing atypical situations, not the least of which is their teenage daughter's conversations with God."[27] However, throughout this study, *Joan of Arcadia* will be analyzed as a drama heavily influenced by supernatural elements which dramatically alter her life as a normal teenager. Thus, it is part of the genre of supernatural teen dramas that also includes *Buffy* and *Roswell*.

Joan Girardi is the central character of this show, and she is a teenager who lives in (you guessed it!) Arcadia, CA. Joan and her family are not particularly religious, but they are portrayed as a typical family in Southern California. Joan is not part of the popular crowd, and often gets in trouble at school. This is problematic since her mother works in the school office. Joan's father is the police chief, and her older brother, Kevin was in a serious car accident and is now confined to a wheelchair. Joan also has a younger brother, Luke, who attends the same high school as Joan. Luke is a bit of a nerd, and is quite self-conscious when it comes to talking to teenage girls, as seen in his interactions with Joan's friend, Grace.[28] Grace Polk is Joan's friend who is targeted by the popular girls in school because she is different and does not conform to their standards of beauty or society's expectations of being female. Adam Rove is an artsy and introverted young man who is dealing with the loss of his

27 "*Joan of Arcadia*." TV.com, 2006 CNET Networks, Inc. www.tv.com

28 Symbolic naming on *Joan of Arcadia* is also seen in reference to Arcadia as a Biblical garden, Luke as the Biblical disciple and brother to Jesus, and Joan's love interest being named Adam as is the first man in the Bible.

mother, and is friends with Joan and Grace. Adam finds out that Joan believes she hears from God in the last episode of the first season, and although he might not believe it entirely, he is supportive of his friend.

The main adolescent characters on *Buffy*, *Roswell*, and *Joan of Arcadia* must face life as normative teens while belonging to the supernatural world as well. The teens on each of these shows are distinctly set apart from mainstream teen culture, in large part because of the supernatural status and abilities of the vampire slayer, alien-human hybrids, and a messenger of God. From Buffy to Liz to Joan, each teen character must confront issues of identity, romance, friendship, and struggles for independence. The fictive teens on these three television series share the quality of being distinctly different from their peers in the normative teen culture because of their involvement in the supernatural world, yet they must still participate in normative teen behavior in order to belong.

Chapter 3

Buffy Summers as Set Apart

The high school years of *Buffy* are based around the idea of normalcy in the life of a teenage girl. The issue of "normalcy" and the "typical" life of an American teenager is constantly at the forefront of this study. Because Buffy is portrayed as abnormal, her life must be contrasted to those teen characters who are engaging in practices identified by dominant culture as standard behavior for teens. As Hersch discusses in *A Tribe Apart*, she describes the adolescents most Americans are familiar with. She writes,

> In most communities outside inner cities, the kids we see appear remarkably like the adolescents we remember from our own childhoods. The ordinary everyday adolescents we see at high school football games, at back-to-school nights, the kids hanging out at the local shopping centers, the ones who load our car at the grocery store, the sitters for the children down the street, the counselors at day camp, the athletes and the cheerleaders and the kids in third-period English class...[29]

The teens that Hersch has described are the "normal teens" – they are living the same experience as the characters on shows like *Buffy*, *The O.C.* and *One Tree Hill*, and even young social media influencers and celebrities of the 2020s. Sunnydale High School is one of the major settings in each season of *Buffy*, and the friendships,

29 Hersch, 14-15.

romances, and family struggles that Buffy faces are all situations that many teenagers confront. However, Buffy's calling as the chosen one, the one girl in all the world selected by fate to fight evil, transforms her into a strong female who is essentially living two lives: one as the normal teen girl, and one as the vampire slayer. Buffy says in more than one episode that she wishes she could be a normal girl who is able to participate in cheerleading, study groups, and high school dances. But fate has pulled her into another role, one where she saves humanity time and time again. Buffy even has a high school sweetheart, a tortured vampire by the name of Angel. She expresses to him in season two her frustrations with not being able to be a normal teenage girl. "Who am I kidding? Dates are things normal girls have. Girls who have time to think about nail polish and facials. You know what I think about? Ambush tactics, beheading. Not exactly the stuff dreams are made of."[30] Buffy is trying to define who she is aside from her calling, and also fulfilling her destiny. She's reconciling two identities, while still grappling with the everyday teen angst.

The dominant friendship of *Buffy the Vampire Slayer* throughout seasons one, two and three is the relationship between Buffy, Xander, and Willow. When Buffy transfers to Sunnydale High from her high school in Los Angeles, she is initially courted by the popular crowd in school, led by Cordelia Chase. However, Buffy chooses to associate with Xander and Willow instead, which is basically social suicide (according to Cordelia). Willow is a horribly self-conscious nerd and Xander is an awkward goofball. Buffy, Willow, and Xander become friends, and Willow and Xander soon learn of Buffy's secret identity. Xander overhears Buffy and Giles (her assigned Watcher and the school librarian) discussing her refusal to accept her calling and Willow is quickly thereafter told of the situation. From here on out, Buffy is joined by her friends in battle.

Giles is cautious of Buffy's identity being found out because he believes it will compromise her safety and the safety of those around her. When an old friend of Buffy's comes to town, Giles suspects Buffy

---

30 *Buffy the Vampire Slayer*, Season 2, Episode 6.

may be using her identity as the slayer to get dates. He questions, "Buffy, you're not by any chance betraying your secret identity just to impress cute boys, are you?"[31] Unfortunately, the fact that this young man, Ford, knows of Buffy's role as the vampire slayer turns ugly when it is discovered that Ford belongs to a "vampire-wannabe" cult. Unbeknownst to Buffy, Ford has been diagnosed with a fatal brain tumor, and he has gathered these followers together in order for the powerful vampires to turn Ford and his friends into vampires. The price for Ford's immortality is Buffy's life, and he has agreed to hand her over to Spike and Drusilla (the villainous vampires) in exchange for being transformed into a vampire and getting a second chance at life by being immortal. Ford says to his followers, "A couple more days and we'll get to do the two things every American teen should have the chance to do. Die young and stay pretty."[32] Just as Ford sends out the message that all American teens should be able to die young and stay pretty, *Buffy the Vampire Slayer* also presents ideas of what it means to be normal teens by contrasting their lives to Buffy's. For instance, Buffy wants to be the homecoming queen and experience her high school prom because that is what normal teens are able to do – even while she is out slaying vampires and saving the world from evil.

Along with these themes of friendship and identity on *Buffy the Vampire Slayer* are the romantic relationships. First and foremost is the romance between Buffy and Angel. Beginning in season two, Buffy is dating Angel who is actually over 200 years old. Being a vampire has allowed Angel to appear to be in his early twenties even when he has seen two centuries pass by. This relationship comes to an explosive end in season two when one moment's happiness costs Angel his soul.

Other major relationship arcs that develop in season two are between Xander and Cordelia, followed by Willow and Oz. Both of these relationships are full of intense emotions, jealousy, and insecurities much like any other teen romance. However, the factors

31 *Buffy the Vampire Slayer,* Season 2, Episode 7.

32 Ibid.

exclusive to the characters on this show complicate their relationships even more. Willow becomes a powerful witch towards the end of season two, and her boyfriend Oz is a werewolf three days out of the month and has to be locked in a cage for everyone's safety. The most "normal teen relationship" here is between the eccentric Xander and the picture-perfect Cordelia. However, even their romance takes a supernatural twist when Xander casts a love spell that goes wrong. Romance for the teens on *Buffy* is anything but normal, as seen by these few examples of the supernatural obstacles that each relationship must overcome.

The last major theme on this series is the parent-child relationship between Buffy and her mother. Buffy's mother, Joyce, is initially in the dark about Buffy's identity as the slayer. She is a single, working mother who wants her daughter to stay out of trouble. This is a problem for Buffy since she is constantly facing evil forces that disrupt school events or prevent her from abiding by the law. Although she means well, Buffy's mom is often in the way of Buffy becoming who she is meant to be. This is a common obstacle for many teenagers, as their parents do not know quite how close to hold them, and when to let them fly free. In season two of the television series, Buffy finally comes clean to her mom about her true identity as the vampire slayer.

> I told you, I'm a vampire slayer. Open your eyes, Mom. What do you think has been going on for the past two years? The fights, the weird occurrences; how many times have you washed blood out of my clothing? And you still haven't figured it out…It never stops. Do you think I chose to be like this? Do you have any idea how lonely it is, how dangerous? I would love to be upstairs watching TV or gossiping about boys, or God, even studying! But I have to save the world. Again.[33]

This statement exposes parents as voluntarily blind or clueless to the real activities and struggles of their children, as indicated by her mother's apparently unquestioning repeated washing of Buffy's

---

33 *Buffy the Vampire Slayer*, Season 2, Episode 22.

blood-stained clothing from her slayer duties. Not surprisingly, Joyce does not take kindly to the news that Buffy is a vampire slayer, and her response is a familiar demonstration of parental authority: placing her teenage daughter on restriction. In fact, she tells Buffy that if she leaves the house then she should never come back. Thus, season two closes with Buffy on a bus heading out of Sunnydale.

As far as paternal support, Buffy's dad is constantly letting her down in the first three seasons of the show. On her 18th birthday, Buffy's father is supposed to take her to an ice show to celebrate, but he backs out at the last minute. This is one of the first times the audience sees Buffy reach out to Giles as a replacement father figure, but he blindly misses the cue. Buffy says, "I mean, if someone were free, they'd take their daughter or their…student…or their Slayer…"[34] Again and again, the audience sees the close father/daughter relationship building between Giles and Buffy. When Giles is fired from the Watcher's Council after this same episode, the reason given is that he is too close to the slayer. Buffy views Giles as an adequate substitute for her own father, and is extremely hurt and betrayed by Giles when he performs a task at the request of the Watcher's Council that requires him to drug Buffy. After this episode, Buffy and Giles begin to repair their relationship, and in a much later episode, Buffy asks Giles to walk her down the aisle at her wedding. Clearly, Buffy views Giles in a paternal way, and Giles is (usually) depicted as a loving example of what a father should be.

34 *Buffy the Vampire Slayer*, Season 2, Episode 22.

Chapter 4

Feeling Otherworldly in Roswell

The idea of alienation as a normative state of being for American teens is again highlighted by the writers of *Roswell*, as the audience meets these literal half-alien creatures who look and act exactly like every other teenager at Roswell High. In a scene from the first episode of season two, the audience sees Max having a counseling session. The psychiatrist says, "Max, I want you to know that however unique you think your problems may be, there are millions of teenagers out there going through exactly what you are going through right now. Let me assure you, this is all normal teenage stuff."[35] Max daydreams and imagines what would happen if he actually responded with the truth: that he is half-alien, but he is quickly jerked back to real life. Although Max's extraterrestrial roots complicate his life, it is true that his alien state of being is parallel to the daily lives of typical fully human teens.

Yet, the alien teens are different in that they, unlike "normal" teens, have superpowers to use in addressing the challenges they face. Late in season three, Liz begins experiencing strange flu-like symptoms combined with a heightened level of electricity and power flowing through her body. She says to Max, "You healed me and now I'm different."[36] Thus, Liz has joined the group of non-normal teens because of her relationship to the individuals

35 *Roswell*, Season 2, Episode 1.

36 *Roswell*, Season 3, Episode 12.

with supernatural powers. This is similar to the experiences of Willow and Xander in *Buffy the Vampire Slayer*, as their friendship with the slayer gives them power even as it complicates their normal teenage existence.

Finally, in his speech at the high school graduation ceremony, Max says, "I'm a member of that group of outsiders. I always knew I was different."[37] Granted, this is something that almost any teenager could claim: being an outsider. In Max's case, his supernatural powers and challenges have left him on the fringes of high school society, never allowing him to fully integrate into the normalcy of teenage life. At the same time, Max experiences the romance, the friendships, the trouble at school, and the family struggles that many teens face during these critical years. It is the element of supernatural power in Max's life that both highlights issues of teen alienation and sets him apart from normal teens; his position as an outsider allows viewers to see that all teens are dealing with their own unique problems, and no one is truly normal.

Friendship is a key theme in this series as well, especially the evolution of the sustaining significance of friendships as the main characters come to terms with the reality of their identities. In season one, the dominant friendships are between Maria and Liz and between Michael and Max. Both friendships are tested by the knowledge that Max, Michael and Isabel are aliens and the fact that more and more people know the truth of their identity. In season two, the friendships between Maria, Liz, Michael, Max and Isabel become more integrated and grow to include the fourth alien-human hybrid teen Tess, and Liz's human friends Alex and Kyle. Finally, in season three, Jesse (Isabel's love interest) is added to the mix and Alex and Tess are no longer present. Also, in this final season, there is an emphasis on the friendship between the human teens – Liz, Maria, and Kyle – and then another emphasis on the friendship between the aliens – Max, Michael, and Isabel – as a separation between aliens and humans appears to be impending.

Not only are friendships tested by the knowledge of secret identities, but the relationship between parent and child is also dam-

37 *Roswell*, Season 3, Episode 18.

aged in many cases on *Roswell*. Parental involvement on *Roswell* is more significant than on *Buffy*, in the sense that many more parents are present in this television series. With *Buffy*, the only parental figures that appear regularly are Joyce and Giles. However, on *Roswell*, the audience routinely sees the teen characters interact with at least six different parental figures. The first parental conflict is between Kyle and Sheriff Valenti, as Kyle sees the search for aliens begin to take over his father's life as it did with his grandfather. As more and more secrets are being kept, the audience sees Maria's relationship with her mother change, as well as the relationship between Liz and her parents and Max and his parents.

For the adult characters on *Roswell*, it seems their children have suddenly decided to make immature decisions that result in them getting into trouble at school and with the law. Even with Max and Isabel's indulgent human parents, there are doubts as to whether their children are living within the limits of the law. In fact, during season three, Max's father pursues an increasingly intense investigation of his son until Max and Isabel tell their parents the truth about their secret identities. Isabel picks up on the tension between Liz and her mother when she overhears a phone conversation between the two. Isabel says to Liz, "The perfect Liz Parker lying to her mom." Liz responds with, "Well, at least she knows what species I am."[38] Although all of the teens have secrets that they hide from their parents, it seems that Liz is able to use the severity of Isabel's secret to justify her own lies.

Finally, romantic relationships are the touchstone of this teen television series. As is the case with most shows in this genre, as Buffy and Angel were the star-crossed lovers in *Buffy the Vampire Slayer*, the main romance on *Roswell* is between the initially mismatched pair of outgoing human Liz and introverted alien Max. However, the supernatural element again plays a dominant role in the romance between Max and Liz. Not only are Max and Liz almost completely unacquainted before he heals her in the café, but they soon find out that their romance is doomed because in his alien re-

38 *Roswell*, Season 1, Episode 6.

ality Max is destined to be with Tess. Also, the supernatural element of Max being an alien adds to the complications of teen romance angst. For instance, in an episode entitled "Sexual Healing" from season one, Max and Liz start to become much more physically intimate. Liz begins getting visions every time she and Max kiss, and soon she has physical evidence of their intimacy. Max says, "Um, Liz, you have a hickey. And it's glowing."[39] Later, Maria comments to Alex in reference to Max and Liz that, "If they actually do it, she'll probably explode."[40] Obviously, this is a problem unique to Max and Liz, but the perils of physical intimacy in teen romances is a situation that many adolescents encounter.

Another important romance throughout all three seasons exists between Michael and Maria. Their relationship is much different from Max and Liz, in that it does not seem to be quite as serious most of the time. Michael is extremely defensive and standoffish and this constantly puts a wall between him and Maria, until the end of season two when Michael finally opens himself up to Maria. Prior to this, Michael and Maria have a short conversation about his inability to express his emotions.

> Michael: I am not completely emotionally retarded. I have feelings.
> Maria: All right, then walk 'em over there and give 'em a workout.[41]

Although there is quite a bit of joking and teasing between them (and insensitive terms to today's standards, to be clear), the intensity of their relationship is obvious even before Michael admits it to Maria – or to himself. In contrast to Max and Liz, Michael and Maria's romance is often in the background, only coming to the forefront during crisis points in their storyline.

---

39 Ibid.

40 *Roswell,* Season 1, Episode 16.

41 *Roswell,* Season 2, Episode 13.

Coming of Age

Chapter 5

What Would Joan Do?

The same series themes that were seen in *Buffy* and *Roswell* are also seen in *Joan of Arcadia*, but in different degrees of significance. Where friendship and teen romance were the main focus points of the other two shows, *Joan of Arcadia's* main focus is on the family. However, the friendships and romance, along with the identity quest that Joan faces, are extremely important as well. The idea of normal teen life is once again a focal point of this television series. In episode six of season one, the audience sees Joan get sucked into the popularity game, as the cheerleaders welcome her into their clique, and Joan leaves Grace and Adam behind. Regardless of how much Joan tries to convince herself that she wants to be an individual, and not be a part of the "in crowd," she is curious to see what it feels like to be on the other side of the divide between popular and outcast. The following verbal exchange between Adam and Joan gives a glimpse into her insecurities regarding to which "group" she belongs.

> Joan: I always thought you'd hate me if I was a cheerleader.
> Adam: No way. Why?
> Joan: 'Cause we're sub-defectives and it would be like deserting the army.[42]

The central friendship on this television series exists between Joan, Grace, and Adam. In episode two, Joan's father says, "These

42 *Joan of Arcadia, Season 1, Episode 6.*

are Joan's new friends? A person of mysterious gender and space boy?"[43] The fact that Joan's father recognizes the unusual appearance in Joan's new friends is a clue that prior to this, Joan was friends with kids who fit more easily into the parental expectations of adolescent friendships. Joan and Grace definitely do not see eye to eye on everything, as evidenced by Grace's comment to Luke in the cheerleading episode when Joan decides to sit with the in-crowd at lunch. Grace tells Luke, "Listen, I normally couldn't care less, but I think your sister needs, like, an intervention or something."[44] Grace is worried that Joan is joining the popular crowd, and as someone who has been targeted for ridicule by these same "popular" girls in the past, Grace is sincerely concerned for Joan's well-being and can only imagine that Joan must be crazy to want to join them.

The friendship between Joan and Adam gradually begins moving toward a romantic relationship, only to be halted when Joan follows God's request to destroy Adam's artwork because she has been instructed to stop Adam's work from being exhibited to prevent him from dropping out of school to focus on his artistic career. However unstable their friendship might have been at this point, by the end of the season, Joan and Adam are definitely a couple. He is the one who sits by her side in the hospital (along with her parents) when she is suffering from Lyme disease and discovers that the past year of her life communicating with God may have just been hallucinations caused by the disease. Adam does not necessarily believe in God speaking to people, but he tells Joan that he believes that she believes it has happened, affirming that he believes *in her*. Adam and Joan's romance is much more innocent and less explicitly sexual than the relationships between Buffy and Angel or Max and Liz. However, this does not mean that their connection is any less intense, an issue that will be explored in more detail in an analysis of Joan's identity quest later on.

Finally, the last major series theme on *Joan of Arcadia* is the relationship between Joan and her family, as well as the overall family dynamics in the Girardi home. *Joan of Arcadia* aired on CBS, a

---

43 *Joan of Arcadia*, Season 1, Episode 6.

44 *Joan of Arcadia*, Season 1, Episode 6.

network well-known for family dramas and not dedicated to the young adult and teen audience like the WB network, so the main focus on this show shifts. Other contributing factors to this additional emphasis on family as well as teen romance and friendships are the Christian framework of Joan's supernatural realm and the establishment of the series in the immediate context of the national tragedy of September 11, 2001.

The family relationship on *Joan of Arcadia* is quite evident: the audience sees the Girardi family sit down to at least one family meal, or interact with one another in the kitchen before work and school in nearly every episode. This would be a rarity on either *Buffy* or *Roswell* because family was not the main focus; teen romance and friendships were the central themes. This is not to say that family relationships were ignored on *Buffy* or *Roswell*, but that family presence, concerns, and issues are much more pronounced and consistent on *Joan of Arcadia*. In a conversation between Kevin and Joan in light of an argument between Joan and her parents, the two siblings discuss the family dynamic. Older (and now wheelchair bound) brother Kevin says, "Joan, here's the thing. Mom likes normal, Dad really likes normal. Before my accident, Luke was all they could handle in the freak-for-a-kid department, now they've got me. You're the only hope for normal."[45] Later, the audience sees a conversation take place between mother and father regarding their concerns about Joan and the pressures of high school. Will (Joan's father) says, "I think I just alienated our daughter for good...How's she going to survive?" Helen (Joan's mother) responds, "She's got a good dad."[46] In these examples (and in many others across the series) family dynamics not only demonstrate effective communication but values of respect and tolerance for individuality within a context of familial love and support.

The supernatural element on this series is something that is in some way familiar to many Americans. Trans-historical vampires and extraterrestrial aliens literally exist "outside" the everyday experience of the viewing audience, whereas belief in a Biblical

45 *Joan of Arcadia*, Season 1, Episode 1.

46 *Joan of Arcadia*, Season 1, Episode 6.

power is both familiar to and reinforces the values of many American teens. Thus, *Joan of Arcadia* is a bit less "out there" than *Buffy* and *Roswell*. According to an article for a special issue of *U.S. News & World Report* in May 2005, *Joan of Arcadia* is less threatening to many viewers, categorizing this series with the likes of *7th Heaven*.

> *Joan of Arcadia* features a teenager who is average in every respect except one: She talks to God, often in the service of solving problems such as whom to vote for in the student council election. But last spring, after God told Joan to offer her boyfriend a gift, and she found a condom in his backpack, she wondered if sex wasn't the gift God had in mind.[47]

This article, which appeared in a special teen issue of the magazine, looks at what teens are really watching on television. *Joan of Arcadia* is included in the section discussing how "some shows try to tip the balance away from sex with spirituality."[48] Instead of being viewed as a science-fiction based teen drama, *Joan of Arcadia* is seen here as more mainstream than *Buffy* or *Roswell* because it is presenting spiritual responses to teen pressures of sex. The other two series often combine the supernatural elements with sexual intimacy, but *Joan of Arcadia* is seen to present a more normative approach to this teen issue.

In analyzing the major series themes for these three teen television dramas, there are commonalities and differences that must be addressed. First, the idea of high school normalcy and the feeling of teenagers on these series identifying as outsiders is a similarity across all three shows. Buffy wants to be involved in the normative teen events of Homecoming and Prom, even while participating in the supernatural world of vampires. Likewise, Liz and Max are presented as outsiders because of Max's connection to the supernatural world and Liz's relationship to Max. On *Roswell*, alienation is seen to be a normal state of being for teens, as many of the teen characters struggle with questions of their own identity. Of course,

47 Betsy Streisand. "What They're Watching: Embracing Hard-Edged Teen Shows as a Chance to Talk." *U.S. News & World Report Mysteries of the Teen Years*, May 2005, Page 67.

48 Ibid.

for Max and Liz, this discovery of identity is complicated by their roles in the supernatural realm. Finally, Joan tells her father that it is normal to be hiding something in high school, because everyone is dealing with questions of who they are and whether or not they belong. This theme of alienation and ideas of high school normalcy are repeated on all three series.

The family situations on each show, however, are markedly different from one teen television series to the next. Parents are largely absent on *Buffy*, with the exception of Buffy's substitute paternal figure, Giles. Buffy's mother is seen in many episodes, but there is largely only surface-level interaction between mother and daughter. And the parents of other focal characters such as Willow and Xander are rarely seen on the series at all. On *Roswell*, there is more frequent interaction between parents and their teen children, but the influence of parents is rarely present. For instance, Liz and Max both keep many secrets from their parents, a situation that becomes more and more apparent as the series goes on. The secrets of teens on this series create remarkable barriers in communication between the teen characters and their parents. Finally, on *Joan of Arcadia* family interaction is a central feature. This is a noticeable difference between this series and *Buffy* and *Roswell* in that Joan's parents are extremely present and influential in her life. Joan has many conversations with her parents about her life as a teenager, and even though she has secrets, her family continues to have a significant impact on her life. This is evidenced by the continuous interactions between Joan and her family, and the constant concern shown by her parents in comments they make to one another throughout the series.

Although *Buffy*, *Roswell*, and *Joan of Arcadia* share many common themes, the way in which each series tackles questions of friendship, romance, identity, and parental influence differs. These series themes are highlighted by the opening montage of each teen television show under analysis here. Also, the use of commercial and alternative music is evidence of the target audience of each show.

Chapter 6

Music & Money – Reaching the Teenagers

In discussing the major themes of these television series, it is important to look at the opening montages of each show. Beginning with *Buffy the Vampire Slayer*, the major themes are seen in glimpses of scenes from the show that are pulled together in this opening assortment of characters, action shots, and key scenes. These opening montages are the window into the themes of *Buffy*, from the key characters to the major relationships of that season, to the role that Buffy must play in the universe. Season one of *Buffy* shows the audience who Buffy was before her calling as the vampire slayer, and who she is during the first year of her playing this role. The core characters remain the same throughout all seasons analyzed herein, with the exception of the addition of Oz in season three.

The opening for *Buffy* begins with the words "who died" from a newspaper article and the word "Buffy" flashing across the screen. The "who died" is representative of the mysterious deaths in Sunnydale, most of which are caused by vampires and demons that Buffy must fight. The audience sees Buffy in various fighting scenes and then a close-up of the historical *Vampyr* book, a history of the creature of the night whom Buffy will spend her life battling against. The audience sees this book in detail in the first episode when Giles reveals himself to Buffy as her watcher, and she is resistant to her calling. The montage also displays clips of Buffy as a cheerleader and dancing at the Bronze (the local all-ages nightclub), and a glimpse of the high school. These are what I classify as the "normal teen" scenes of the opening montage of *Buffy*. They give the audience a glimpse into one of Buffy's dual roles: an adolescent high school girl.

Other character profiles follow as the montage continues, beginning with Xander and Willow, then Angel, Cordelia and Giles. The evil characters of this season are shown in clips of the Master (a very old and very evil vampire whom Buffy fights at the end of season one) and someone rising from the dead in the cemetery (a frequent scene in the series). The final scene here is of Giles, Xander, Willow and Buffy gathering weapons and leaving the library, and the last clip is of Buffy standing alone after a victory at the Bronze. This final scene is key, because it showcases Buffy as someone who may have friends and a normal life outside of slaying, but in the end she is always fighting alone.

The major change to season two's opening montage reflects the focal relationship of this season as the romance between Buffy and Angel grows. The montage for the third season demonstrates major changes from the previous two season openings. It begins with new fighting scenes of Buffy with her recently discovered co-slayer, Faith. One critical scene from the final episodes from season two is added to this opening montage as well. The scene is of Buffy and Angel kissing in the last episode of season two in which Buffy must kill Angel to save the world. Also, Willow's boyfriend, Oz is added as a main character in this opening. Finally, the ending here is a new scene of the main group working together, as they carry a rocket launcher down the hallway in preparation for battle. Following this is the final scene of Buffy alone in a battle at the Bronze. Again, the key is that Buffy is alone in this final clip, just as she was in the previous two seasons.

The music of *Buffy the Vampire Slayer* is extremely indicative of the time period during which this series originally aired. Like fashion and slang, trendy or popular music is constantly changing. Granted, the artists that were prominent on this show are not necessarily well-known today. However, the music was extremely in tune to the teen and young adult audience of this show and many of the bands whose songs were played in the background (or who actually played in a "live" show on *Buffy* at the Bronze) were recognizable to the viewers. According to Nancy Holder, the author of *The Watcher's Guide Volume 2,* "the music of *Buffy* appears in the background of scenes for dramatic impact, appears in recorded form as an integrated part of the characters' lives, or can be part of a "live" performance by fictional or real bands, usually in the Bronze."[49]

The theme song of *Buffy the Vampire Slayer* is performed by Nerfherder, a band from Santa Barbara, California that formed in 1994. Their song soon became the anthem of *Buffy*, but the interesting thing here is that there are no lyrics to the song at all. It is an instrumental piece of music that represents the fighting, the action, and the constant movement in this series. I would argue that the wordless action music allows for the clips of the show to speak louder than lyrics to a theme song. At the same time, certain songs playing in episodes of *Buffy the Vampire Slayer* contain lyrics that tell the story of the characters at a given point in the series. One such memorable song played during this series is "Wild Horses" by the Sundays. This song is playing when Angel walks into the prom in season three. After telling Buffy that he does not want her life to be with him, he still shows up at the prom because he recognizes how much this teenage rite of passage means to Buffy. The song encapsulates the relationship between Buffy and Angel perfectly, as the words capture the dramatic tension between these two characters and the love that will survive even if their relationship ends.

> I watched you suffer a dull, aching pain
> Now you decided to show me the same
> No sweeping exits or offstage lines,
> Can make me feel bitter or treat you unkind.
> *[Chorus:]*
> Wild Horses
> Couldn't drag me away,
> Wild, wild horses,
> Couldn't drag me away…[50]

---

49 Nancy Holder et.al. *The Watcher's Guide Volume 2*. New York: Pocket Books, 2000. Page 455.

50 A-Z Lyrics, "Wild Horses by the Sundays." June 24, 2006. www.stlyrics.com

Although Buffy and Angel have caused each other pain, they cannot tear themselves away from one another. And because Angel realizes both his devotion to Buffy and that he wants Buffy to have a better, more normal life than she could have with him, he leaves town. The only way that they can truly separate themselves from one another is through physical distance. Even as Angel tells Buffy he must leave, he asks, "You still my girl?" And Buffy answers, "Always."[51] The music in *Buffy the Vampire Slayer* often captures the mood of the moment or the episode, and in this specific case, it describes the emotions of the characters. Music is a powerful tool of characterization and reiteration of the themes of the series and of the specific episodes.

As with *Buffy*, looking at the opening montage of each season of *Roswell* allows for a more focused analysis of the dominant themes of this teen television series. Season one's opening montage begins with a quick snapshot of the desert followed by an image of the newspaper story about the Roswell crash. We then see Max walking alone in the desert, followed by the silhouettes of Max, Isabel, and Michael walking together in the desert. Next are glimpses of Liz working at the CrashDown Café, followed by the one image that will be in all three seasons' openings: Max looks through the restaurant window from outside, as Liz gazes back at him from inside the café. This scene shows the audience (especially since it appears in the opening of all three seasons) that the relationship between Max and Liz is the dominant one in this series, and that there are obstacles between them, as represented by the window.

We later see Max and Liz at the window again, followed by the scene in the café when Max heals Liz and then leaves. Next come the character shots of Liz, Max, Isabel, and Maria. The bond between Max, Isabel, and Michael is reiterated with an image of the three of them from episode one at the crash re-enactment standing at the fence watching the fake spaceship crash into the ground. This is followed by the remaining character shots of Michael, Alex, Kyle, and Sheriff Valenti.

---

51 *Buffy the Vampire Slayer*, Season 3, Episode 17.

The final scenes of this opening montage are focused on Max and Liz. The audience again sees an image of Max and Liz at the CrashDown Café window. Max is peering in and Liz is looking out at him. Finally, the montage closes with a clip of Liz standing in the school hallway alone. This is a glimpse into the final episode of the season, when Max joins Isabel, Michael, and Tess in following their destinies as a foursome, while Liz is left all alone.

The opening montage of season two is initially quite similar to that of the first season. One additional scene is added of Max, Michael, and Isabel listening to the story of their past as told to them by Max and Isabel's mother at the end of season one. Later in the opening montage, the word "ROSWELL" flashes across the screen and the audience again sees Liz and Max at the window of the café. The final scene in this montage is of Max, Michael, Isabel, Liz, Maria and Alex at the cliff where they often meet to discuss pertinent issues. Essentially, the changes made for season two's opening are indicative of the major relationships, and the characters that will make an impact during these episodes.

Finally, season three is quite different from seasons one and two, as more characters are included and the storyline shifts. Interestingly, the series switched from WB network to UPN at the beginning of its final season, which could account for some of the changes. It begins with a flash of outer space, followed by the same newspaper story clipping seen in the previous seasons. Next is the new split screen of Max, Michael, and Isabel followed by a clip of these three individuals plus Tess in the Granolith chamber which was a pivotal scene from season two for the alien-human hybrids. The major emphasis here is still on Max, Michael, and Isabel's relationship as we see their silhouettes walking through the desert together.

A major change from the previous seasons is an equal emphasis on the human teens of *Roswell*, as the audience sees clips of Liz, Maria, and Kyle followed by a scene of the three of them at the CrashDown Café together. Again, the Max and Liz window scene is included, followed by the word "ROSWELL" written in interesting characters that are the same as the book in which the alien-human hybrids' history is recorded. The word "ROSWELL" then changes into regular letters, and we see two hands reaching for each other. Obviously, the romance between Max and Liz will remain a dominant storyline in this season, as a clip of them kissing and then hugging is shown.

The scenes for this season's opening continue with a focus on a second romantic relationship between Maria and Michael, as two clips of them together are shown, followed by a close-up of Michael. This is followed by the final clip of the six main characters of this season: Max, Michael, Isabel, Liz, Maria, and Kyle. They are all outside of the pod chamber after Tess has left in season two and Alex is dead. Each of the dominant relationships are displayed in season three's opening, along with images that show Max's leadership and the continuation of the identity quest of Max, Michael, and Isabel.

Just as with *Buffy the Vampire Slayer*, the opening montages of each season of *Roswell* provide a window into the series themes. The major themes are quite similar, as the idea of normalcy in the lives of high school teenagers plays a strong role in this series as well. Other crossover themes include the romantic relationships between the teens, the central friendships among this group, and the identity quests of those who are deemed outside the norm. The identity quests of Max, Isabel, and Michael are at the forefront of this series.

Music plays a key role in telling the story of the main characters on *Roswell*, as the power of the theme song is seen more clearly on this show than possibly any other show of its genre. The theme song "Here With Me" was a major commercial rock hit performed by Dido (1999) and was assumedly well-familiar to teen viewers. The lyrics illustrate the romance between Liz and Max, and the connections that Max, Michael and Isabel have to their life, family and friends on Earth. In illustrating the relationship between Max and Liz, the words tell the story of two people in love with one another to the point of not wanting to forget one single moment of their lives together. The lyrics are as follows:

> I didn't hear you leave
> I wonder how am I still here
> And I don't want to move a thing
> It might change my memory
> *[Chorus:]*
> Oh I am what I am
> I'll do what I want
> But I can't hide
> I won't go
> I won't sleep
> I can't breathe
> Until you're resting here with me
> I won't leave
> I can't hide
> I cannot be
> Until you're resting here with me
> I don't want to call my friends
> They might wake me from this dream
> And I can't leave this bed
> Risk forgetting all that's been[52]

The key line here is "I am what I am" because it conveys the basic message of *Roswell*: embrace who you are, and other people will love you for it. "I can't hide" and "I cannot be until you're resting here with me" are both applicable to Max and Liz's relationship, as they form an unbreakable bond of shared self-knowledge that withstands Max's brief romance with Tess which results in the birth of his son.

"I am what I am" is a declaration of identity being both recognized and implicitly under challenge. The real self must be hidden in order to protect their identity, yet neither Liz nor Max wants to change who they are. At the same time, they are both seeking to be

52 Dido. "Here With Me" song lyrics. www.azlyrics.com

valued and wanting to establish a connection with someone who knows the "real" self. These identity issues that Max and Liz face as they form a romantic bond are recognizable and relatable to many real teens. As adolescents attempt to discover who they are and who they want to be, they are often forming bonds with their peers and romantic interests, which complicates their own identity quests as is the case with Liz and Max throughout the series.

The opening montage of season one of *Joan of Arcadia* is much different than *Buffy* and *Roswell*. There are less scenes of the show itself and more images of the characters. The representations in this opening montage begin with the words "Joan of Arcadia" followed by dated pictures of world events or famous people throughout history. The link to the series here is that the title, *Joan of Arcadia*, is clearly a play on the historical figure, Joan of Arc. Joan of Arc was a woman who lived during the 15th century in France, who claimed to receive visions from God. She was burnt at the stake as a result of the tension between France and Britain during the Hundred Years War.[53] The martyr theme first mentioned in connection with *Buffy the Vampire Slayer* is seen here as well. Joan Girardi is portrayed as a martyr, just as Joan of Arc sacrificed her life for her religious beliefs. On *Joan of Arcadia*, God asks Joan to give up certain things in her own life in order to carry out his instructions on Earth. Joan must be willing to give up life as she knows it to truly be a messenger of God on this teen series.

Another important characteristic of the opening montage of *Joan of Arcadia* is that like *Roswell*, it has an extremely powerful theme song: the 1995 popular commercial rock hit, "One of Us" by Joan Osborne.

> If God had a name what would it be?
> And would you call it to his face?
> If you were faced with him in all his glory
> What would you ask if you had just one question?

53 "Joan of Arc" Wikipedia, Updated June 2006. http://en.wikipedia.org/wiki/Joan_of_Arc.

I – And yeah, yeah, God is great
Yeah, yeah, God is good
Yeah, yeah, yeah-yeah-yeah
What if God was one of us?
Just a slob like one of us
Just a stranger on the bus
Tryin' to make his way home?
If God had a face what would it look like?
And would you want to see if, seeing meant
That you would have to believe in things like heaven
And in Jesus and the saints, and all the prophets?
Back up to heaven all alone
No, nobody calling on the phone
No, just tryin' to make his way home
Nobody calling on the phone
'Cept for the Pope maybe in Rome[54]

The lyrics of this song speak directly to the spiritual questions that *Joan of Arcadia* is asking its audience. First, what if God was just an average person on the street? Also, would you want to meet God, if meeting God meant that you must believe? And lastly, if you had one question to ask God, what would it be? These all revolve around huge cultural questions of faith and religion and spirituality. Instead of focusing on the supernatural elements in terms of monsters, witchcraft, aliens and supernatural powers, *Joan of Arcadia* focuses on the persistent questions surrounding faith in general. Yet, these large questions can also be understood to embody a double meaning for teen viewers: questions of identity and the struggle to find one's own place in the world. In the lyrics of this song are questions of being alienated by having the real self hidden from or not recognized by others. Implicit in this song are also feelings of many teens, and definitely the opinion of Joan in regards to a skepticism or negation of larger truths and goodness that may or may not exist in the world.

---

54 https://genius.com/Joan-osborne-one-of-us-lyrics, Accessed December 4, 2025.

Following the images of the historical Joan of Arc, the montage then focuses on the central characters of the television series, beginning with a clip of Joan in the hallway of her high school. This is followed by a series of clips of the main characters of the series. Interestingly enough, each single character picture is followed by a scene which links the previous character with the next. The first character shown is Will Girardi, Joan's father, first alone and then with his wife, Helen. This is followed by a scene in which Helen is with her daughter, Joan and then a clip of Joan herself. We then see Kevin and Luke, followed by a family scene outside of the house they share, in visual establishment of the nuclear family household.

As with *Buffy* and *Roswell*, the conclusion of this opening montage is quite important, and provides a clue as to what the focus of this show will be. I believe the family scene in front of the house is crucial, along with the final clip which is a close-up of Joan. This brings everything full circle with the initial scene of Joan in the hallway of her high school alone. In many ways, the montage for *Joan of Arcadia* is like the final clip of Buffy in the opening of her show, in which she is always fighting alone in the end. Likewise, Joan alone has been selected by God to do his will, a mission which often isolates her or places her on the outside of her family. Thus, the montage begins and ends with Joan, with the bulk of the montage scenes showing the links between Joan and her family.

The series themes are directly tied to the music that is played on *Joan of Arcadia*. The powerful lyrics of the theme song ask the main questions of this television series. This same use of powerful lyrics, contained within popular teen music of the time, is the idea behind most of the songs played on this series. For example, the audience hears songs by pop artists Avril Lavigne and 3 Doors Down, both of whom had Top 100 hits in the year that *Joan of Arcadia* played their tunes. The difference here is that many of the songs on *Joan of Arcadia* could be recognized by both teens and adults, such as "Time Has Come Today" by Joan Jett[55] and "La Vie En Rose" by Cyndi Lauper.[56] In *Buffy* and *Roswell*, songs used in specific episodes were a

55 *Joan of Arcadia*, Season 1, Episode 9.

56 *Joan of Arcadia*, Season 1, Episode 22.

bit more "alternative" and more familiar to the teen audience. Yet, the music on all three shows is most readily identifiable by the teen and young adult audience of these television series. The montage of each of these three television series allows the viewer to have a snapshot view of what will be the focus of each show. *Buffy*, *Roswell*, and *Joan of Arcadia* have compelling opening montages that inform the viewer of the combination of normative teen culture and the involvement of chosen teens from each show in the supernatural world. Both *Buffy* and *Joan of Arcadia* focus on the chosen status of the title characters, while *Roswell* focuses largely on the relationship between Max and Liz. The supernatural elements of these shows highlight the distinctive nature of teens in America, and the many ways in which they are both separate from and expected to play a part in dominant culture. The powerful theme songs in *Roswell* and *Joan of Arcadia* emphasize this theme of identity and questions of faith and connections to the supernatural world. The opening montages and use of powerful music in these supernatural teen television dramas provide evidence to the argument that teens are set apart and are each called to fulfill an unique destiny. At the same time, teens are expected to participate in the normative adolescent culture which would be incomplete without the influence of consumerism on America's teen culture.

Product placement and pop culture references on *Buffy*, *Roswell*, and *Joan of Arcadia* are indicative of the largely teen audience that each show is speaking to, and the type of viewer response the writers of each show are hoping to invoke. Pop culture references and product placement are quite abundant on *Roswell*. Early on in season one, the audience witnesses Maria singing along to Christina Aguilera's 1999 hit song "Genie in a Bottle." Later in this season, we see Michael and Max drinking Pepsi and Sprite on their lunch break at school. In episode six of season one, Michael and Maria get stuck in a motel room together. Michael goes in search of a vending machine and comes back with snacks: Chips Ahoy cookies, Doritos chips, and Tabasco sauce. Tabasco is a product repeatedly shown in the series because it is a favorite condiment of the alien-human hybrids. It is said that Max, Michael, Isabel and Tess like their food to be extra spicy yet extra sweet at the same time. Much to the disgust of the human characters (and likely some viewers), they proceed to put Tabasco sauce on everything from French fries to pancakes.

As Alissa Quart discusses in her book, *Branded: The Buying and Selling of Teenagers*, brand marketing of consumer products at junior high schools, high schools, and colleges was extremely prevalent in the United States in the early 2000s. "One hundred and fifty school districts in twenty-nine states have Pepsi and Coke contracts. Textbooks regularly mention Oreo cookies, and math problems contain Nike logos."[57] Branded consumer items are so prominent in the everyday lives of real teens that it only adds to the realism of the series when *Roswell* embraces this aspect of teen life. On the other hand, the fact that Max and Michael drink Pepsi and Sprite definitely did not harm the sales of these products.

And so the pop culture references just keep coming on *Roswell*, as Liz refers to Isabel as the Elle McPherson of Roswell High in the first season. Also, in season two the group of teens travel to Las Vegas, in an episode entitled "Viva Las Vegas" – an obvious allusion to the famous song of the same title by Elvis Presley. Finally, in season three there is an entire episode built around the drink Snapple. In subsequent episodes, Maria often asks for a Snapple to drink whenever she visits Michael at his house. These are just a sample of the products and pop culture references seen throughout this series, and it is quite clear that advertising and marketing products in these episodes is a powerful tactic within the teen entertainment industry.

Product placement is also crucial in *Buffy*, along with the pop culture references that characters toss out at random times during the show's seven season run. In season two, episode six "Halloween" the audience sees Buffy drinking a Diet Dr. Pepper at school. Later in the same season, Buffy is contemplating what she will do once the big battle of the episode is done in "What's My Line Part 2." Buffy tells Kendra, "When this is over, I'm thinking pineapple

57 Quart, 11.

pizza and teen movie fest. Possibly something from the Ringwald oeuvre,"[58] referencing the 1980s teen movies starring Molly Ringwald, from *Pretty in Pink* to *The Breakfast Club* to *Sixteen Candles*. In the "Homecoming" episode from season three, Cordelia tells Buffy how she feels about Xander. "He kind of grows on you. Like a Chia Pet."[59] This is yet another reference to a popular consumer item of the time. Finally, in "Graduation Day Part 1" from season three, Willow sadly says, "Oh trusty soda machine, I push you for a root beer, you give me a Coke."[60] These are just a small sample of the many pop culture and product placements in this series. Quart discusses the role of teens in consumer culture, arguing that for teens, "the new consumerism is marked by a division between an adolescent desire to emulate adult consumption and the limitations of adolescence itself, financial and emotional."[61] The use of commonplace elements of consumer culture not only allows teen viewers to draw parallels between their lives and the lives of Buffy and the gang, it also encourages the viewers to spend their limited financial resources in certain ways. As they see specific products and hear references to familiar bands, movies, and celebrities, the real teen viewers may make consumer decisions based on the choices of their favorite teen characters.

Finally, the presence of consumer culture on *Joan of Arcadia* is much less frequent and less blatant than on *Buffy* and *Roswell*. *Joan of Arcadia* does contain a few pop culture references in season one, beginning with the title of episode six, "Bringeth It On," an obvious play on the popular 2000 teen cheerleading film, "Bring It On," starring Kirsten Dunst and Gabrielle Union. Another pop culture reference is found in episode five, when Helen refers to well-known afternoon television talk show host of the time, Dr. Phil. Of note, both of these references to popular culture are familiar to both teens and adults. In contrast to the frequent product

58 *Buffy the Vampire Slayer*, Season 2, Episode 10.

59 *Buffy the Vampire Slayer*, Season 3, Episode 5.

60 *Buffy the Vampire Slayer*, Season 3, Episode 21.

61 Quart, 31.

placement on *Roswell*, there are no blatant product placements on *Joan of Arcadia*, however since this was a primetime Friday night series on a major network, targeted commercials undoubtedly made up for the lack of product placement within the series itself. *Joan of Arcadia* manages to connect with teen viewers via pop culture references and current popular music even as the series drops more deliberate solicitation of teen consumerism in favor of maintaining its broader family audience. The major series themes of friendship, romance, and discord between parents and their teenage children are multifaceted on the supernatural teen television series under analysis here, because of the fact that each of the main teen characters has been chosen to fulfill a supernatural calling in addition to just living a normal adolescent life.

These major series themes are the common threads that tie *Buffy*, *Roswell*, and *Joan* together. They form a particular type of genre, a subset of teen television dramas from the late 20th and early 21st centuries in homes across America. Adult construction of these teen series gives viewers a scripted version of what the adult producers, writers, and creators want to portray as teen reality. Yet, the interpretive community of teen viewers that are the audience of each of these shows act as the judges of how "real" the issues and circumstances of these teen characters truly are. It is the combination of supernatural elements and normative teen culture that truly distinguishes *Buffy*, *Roswell*, and *Joan of Arcadia* as unique teen television dramas.

In the post-9/11 environment, television programming shifted away from topics addressing the unknown, and in this context, *Joan of Arcadia* can be seen as a transitional show, falling between the supernatural worlds of *Buffy* and *Roswell* and the later post-9/11 teen dramas such as *The O.C.*, *One Tree Hill*, and *Veronica Mars*. *Buffy* and *Roswell* dealt with supernatural worlds that are unfamiliar to many viewers, but *Joan of Arcadia* looks at the spiritual realm of Judeo-Christian tradition that many American viewers are familiar with, even if they are not personally believers of this theology. This makes *Joan of Arcadia* much more accessible to a family audience, as well as less threatening to the belief systems of potential viewers.

Instead of questioning the ideas of normalcy and making the main characters supernatural thereby highlighting the differences between outsiders and normal teens, teen television series such as *The O.C.*, *One Tree Hill*, and *Veronica Mars* began to look a lot more like early teen dramatic series such as *Beverly Hills, 90210*. Viewers saw a return to the focus on normative (and often privileged) white teenagers dealing with everyday problems of romance, friendship, and high school. However, *Buffy*, *Roswell* and *Joan of Arcadia* incorporate storylines that focus on normative teen culture but are also influenced by the supernatural callings of the main characters of each teen television series.

Essentially, it is the participation in normative teen culture by the main teen characters of *Buffy*, *Roswell*, and *Joan of Arcadia* coupled with the supernatural abilities and/or connections of these fictive teens that allow each of these shows to explore issues of adolescent identity, friendships, romance, and familial relationships in much more depth than other teen television dramas. The incorporation of these normative teen struggles as well as the use of commercial music and symbols of consumer culture sparks a sense of familiarity among the teen viewers. At the same time, the supernatural "otherness" of these teen characters speaks to the alienation of real teens in America. What these distinctive teen characterizations have to say to and about their real teen viewers becomes clear in the close analyses of specific characters that are the subjects of the next chapter.

Jenn Burton

Chapter 7

This Is Who We Are: Central Characters as Surreal Teens

Characters are truly what distinguish one show from another in the teen drama television genre and are responsible for the connections that viewers have with each show. The cultural importance of presenting a certain image of what normative teen behavior means whether we're analyzing newspaper clippings from the 1950s or teen television series from the 1990s or TikTok influencers of the 2020s, we are looking at the physical and emotional changes and the societal pressures that tie every member of this subculture in America together in a collective experience. In her study of adolescents, Patricia Hersch goes in search of the real teens who are being labeled by the adults studying adolescence at the time. Hersch states,

> Styles change, music changes, but the shadow of a mustache on a thirteen-year-old boy, the rough-and-tumble pickup basketball games, the groups of giggling girls, the lingering kisses of young lovers, the Homecoming celebration, the prom, graduation, all look similar to what we recall. There is a confounding lack of congruence between what adults see and what we are told is true. What constitutes a 'normal" adolescence in today's world may or may not be camouflaged by appearances.[62]

62 Hersch, 15.

In keeping with Hersch's argument, the normative qualities of teens in everyday experiences are being overshadowed by the theories of "bad kids" of this new generation and the societal images of adolescents as deviants. Yet, Hersch sees the reality that many of today's teens are quite similar to adolescents of the past. The normative behaviors of teens have not changed so drastically that they are unrecognizable to the adults who once were teens themselves and are now part of the dominant culture.

Instead of being set apart from adult culture in the most basic of ways, David Elkind, professor at Tufts University, and specialist in the field of adolescent psychology, contends that teens are forced to deal with adult issues but are extremely unprepared for these grown-up demands. Elkind claims,

> Adolescents are now seen as a 'niche market' whose emerging sexuality, need for peer-group approval, and search for idols can all be manipulated to motivate them to buy a variety of goods from clothing to CDs. High schools that once afforded many different adult-organized activities have become, in many communities, centers for theft, violence, sex, and substance abuse. In a variety of ways, therefore, the world of adolescents today is continuous with, rather than separate from, the world of adults.[63]

In contrast to Hersch's argument, Elkind sees a real transition from what teens used to be and what teens are today. He argues that the consumerism that has taken over since the 1960s has caused a gradual shift in the societal demands for adolescents to operate in the world of adults. Both Hersch and Elkind are arguing in favor of the existence of a normal adolescence in today's world. While they do not agree on the way in which cultural pressures affect how teens are treated by dominant culture, both recognize normative qualities that characterize teen culture. While Hersch sees the symbols of teen culture as separating adolescents from mainstream adult culture, Elkind views teen culture

---

63 David Elkind, *All Grown Up and No Place to Go: Teenagers in Crisis*. (Massachusetts, Da Capo Press, 1998), 7.

as bleeding into the dominant culture because of societal pressure for teens to cope with adult issues. The recognition of adolescent culture as containing normative qualities is important to my own argument, because these normative behaviors and symbols of teen culture are both represented by the teen characters on *Buffy, Roswell,* and *Joan of Arcadia* as well as the real teen viewers of the shows. Likewise, the celebrities of TikTok and YouTube influence the real teens of the 2020s and have become idols and icons to today's adolescents.

In shows like *Buffy the Vampire Slayer*, *Roswell,* and *Joan of Arcadia*, it is the combination of normative characteristics and supernatural connections of the central characters that appeal to the real teen audience. As cultural media critic Lynn Schofield Clark points out, "Today's young people want to be a part of something that is bigger than themselves: they want a destiny, a calling, a challenge that is ultimately worthy of their time and energy."[64] Thus, the supernatural powers of the central characters on these shows allow real teens to imagine their own higher calling – a special place in the world for each of them. Buffy, Liz and Joan alternately reject and embrace the cultural values of what it means to be a teen girl by representing normative qualities of adolescent females. At the same time, they are all specifically chosen for a purpose in the supernatural world as well.

Buffy the Vampire Slayer: The Chosen One

In an article from Teen *TV: Genre, Consumption, Identity* entitled "Chosen Ones: Reading the Contemporary Teen Heroine", Jenny Bavidge writes

> By defining herself against certain categories of girlhood and re-creating those which are still haunting popular culture, Buffy formulates new versions of old myths. She becomes a contemporary manifestation of the teen heroine, often confronted with many of the same issues, albeit within different context...But the most radical movement the show-

64 Clark, 69.

> makes is its explicit engagement with femininity as performance and its questioning of the traditional narrative trajectories of female heroism.[65]

As Bavidge and other scholars such as Lynn Schofield Clark have argued, Buffy is seen as a teen heroine, a girl who defies the narrative of female teens as victims. However, Buffy also envies the normal lives of other adolescent girls, most often in the storylines involving Cordelia Chase. Many times, Buffy's circumstances are in opposition and contradictory to Cordelia's priorities. Buffy constantly has one foot in each world, and the balancing act is exhausting for her at times. Buffy is a heroine for her generation of teenage viewers, despite the girl-poisoning culture that Mary Pipher discusses in *Reviving Ophelia*, in which she discusses the media images of perfectly thin adolescent and young adult females. Her strength and power are what set Buffy apart in the supernatural world, not her beauty or clothing size. Pipher writes, "As I looked at the culture that girls enter as they come of age, I was struck by what a girl-poisoning culture it was…America today limits girls' development, truncates their wholeness and leaves many of them traumatized."[66] From body shaming to pressures to have sex before they're ready to self-injury and eating disorders, teenage girls from the 1950s through the 2020s can all relate to the societal pressure to be thin, beautiful and quiet. In a media-saturated world where teen audiences in the 1990s saw horror films such as *Scream* and *I Know What You Did Last Summer* feature the female teen victim who is tormented and chased, Buffy comes on the scene with a strength and a destiny that distinguishes her as a girl warrior.

In certain episodes of *Buffy*, the audience sees a glimpse of what the typical teen girl should be: physically weak and in need of male protection, attractive, loved by her peers, and obedient to her parents and authority figures. For example, in episode six of season two, entitled, "Halloween," the residents of Sunnydale who have purchased their Halloween costumes from a specific shop in

---

65 zine." *Teen TV: Genre, Consumption, Identity*. Edited by Glyn Davis and Kay Dickinson (London: British Film Institute, 2004), 49.

66 Mary Pipher, *Reviving Ophelia: Saving the Selves of Adolescent Girls*. (New York: Ballantine Books, 1994), xiii.

town turn into the monsters, ghosts, and characters that they have dressed up as. For Buffy, this means she literally becomes an 18th century girl. The first element here is the fact that Buffy has chosen this costume to impress Angel, because he lived during this time period and associated with women whose entire existence was built around their ability to dress well and marry young (hopefully catching a wealthy man). Buffy, as the 18th century girl, tells Xander, "I was brought up a proper lady, I wasn't meant to understand things. I'm just meant to look pretty, and then someone nice will marry me. Possibly a baron."[67] Although the writers of this show are using a two-hundred-year age gap to exaggerate this idea of girlhood, it is possible that this is not such a foreign concept in today's world.

It is a common cultural model in America today that girls are meant to be more fragile than boys, they are not supposed to "understand" the complexities of life, and adolescent girls are not expected to be warriors. As feminist writer and founder of the National Organization for Women, Betty Friedan, argues in *The Feminine Mystique*, the cultural model of femininity restricts women to the role of subservient housewife.

> Beneath the sophisticated trappings, it simply makes certain concrete, finite, domestic aspects of feminine existence – as it was lived by women whose lives were confined, by necessity, to cooking, cleaning, washing, bearing children – into a religion, a pattern by which all women must now live or deny their femininity.[68]

However insignificant this cultural model may appear to be today, it is, in fact, still in existence in American culture. Ideas regarding the femininity of adolescent girls still reflect the major philosophy behind a cultural model such as the feminine mystique which is founded on the belief that women are in need of male protection and are incapable of taking care of themselves financially, physically, and emotionally. This is displayed in the cultural insistence on little boys playing in the mud from an early age, where little girls

---

67 *Buffy the Vampire Slayer*, Season 2, Episode 6.

68 Betty Friedan, *The Feminine Mystique* (New York: W.W. Norton & Company, Inc., 1963), 43.

are dressed up in frilly outfits and told to stay out of the dirt. Yet, as Joan Jacobs Brumberg discusses in *The Body Project: An Intimate History of American Girls*,

> Contemporary girls seem to have more autonomy, but their freedom is laced with peril. Despite sophisticated packaging, many remain emotionally immature, and that makes it all the more difficult to withstand the sexually brutal and commercially rapacious society in which they grow up.[69]

In contrast to the females that Brumberg describes, Buffy challenges these cultural definitions of female characteristics, as she fights to save the world from demons and forces of evil.

Even as she challenges the cultural model of femininity, Buffy does not completely reject the cultural expectations of teen girls. In many episodes involving typical events of high school life such as extracurricular activities or sports, Buffy is quite envious of normal teen girls. In the "Homecoming" episode from season three, the audience sees that Buffy wants to have some semblance of the life she lived as the popular cheerleader before she was chosen as the slayer. As Buffy argues with one of the popular girls vying for Homecoming Queen, Buffy counters against the notion that she doesn't need Homecoming Queen because she's already the slayer. Buffy retorts, "This is all I do. This is what my life is. You wouldn't understand. I just thought, Homecoming Queen. I could pick up a yearbook someday and say, I was there. I went to high school, I had friends, and for one moment I got to live in the world...."[70] Buffy Summers is seeking validation that, vampire slaying aside, she is a particular kind of teen girl. Granted, she was predestined to save the world as the one girl in all the world chosen to fight dark forces, but at her core, she is an adolescent female attempting to find her place in the world. Participating in the teen culture at Sunnydale High School is extremely important to Buffy. She wants to be recognized in this teen culture, not just in the slayer culture that takes her away from adolescent normalcy.

---

69 Joan Jacobs Brumberg, *The Body Project: An Intimate History of American Girls* (New York: Vintage Books, 1997), 197.

70 *Buffy the Vampire Slayer*, Season 3, Episode 5.

But, as Hersch contends, adolescent normalcy is difficult to define. She writes:

> Whatever constituted 'normal adolescence' for 'regular kids' today had been eclipsed by an emphasis on the sensational. There was a huge gap in the knowledge so necessary not only for parents, but also for society. If the statistics were true, we needed to understand better how the sensational issues might play out in a young person's day-to-day life.[71]

Adolescent normalcy is not a concept easily defined, because it is comprised of the cultural view of adolescence and the actual characteristics of ordinary teens in America. These normative characteristics can be seen in the everyday behaviors of the average high school student, from talking with friends to being branded in a certain way by consumer items to the language of teens. Hersch notes that oftentimes the normative qualities of teens are ignored in favor of examining the more dramatic issues that some teens must face. For David Elkind, the language markers of teen culture are significant in the transition from childhood to adolescence. "In many ways, moving from the culture of childhood to the culture of adolescence is like moving from one society to another. The abrupt change in the language as well as in the rules and expectations regarding conduct can lead to another variety shock – peer shock."[72] Just as with any subculture, a certain behavior or physical appearance identifies an individual's association with a group. For adolescents, not belonging to a specific group leaves many adolescents feeling alienated. Thus, adolescent normalcy can be defined by those characteristics that connect teens from many subgroups under the umbrella of a distinct subculture of teens. Elkind's recognition of the negative effects of not belonging is an important concept to understand when looking at adolescent normalcy and the everyday experience of teens in America.

Buffy is constantly challenging the historical definition of what a slayer should be, because she wants to be a normal teen girl while she is fulfilling her role as the slayer. This is brought to light when

71 Hersch, 15.

72 Elkind, 81.

Buffy first arrives in Sunnydale and Giles is taken aback by Buffy's attitude and her determination to have a social life outside of slaying. When the new slayer, Kendra appears on the scene, it is clear that she does not approve of Buffy's lifestyle as the slayer. In season two, Kendra has been called to be the slayer because, technically, Buffy died for a few minutes before Xander revived her when she faced the Master in season one. Kendra was taken from her family at an early age, and her entire life revolves around slaying and training. She has no friends and does not remember her family. This is in stark contrast to Buffy, because she not only has friends and family, but she involves them in her life as the slayer. Even Spike, the resident evil vampire of season two, remarks on the lifestyle choices of Buffy as different than other slayers before her. "A slayer with family and friends. That sure as hell wasn't in the brochure."[73] Kendra is also awed by – if initially disapproving of – Buffy's choice to involve her friends in slayer battles. Kendra says to Buffy, "The things you do and have, I was taught distract from my calling. Friends, school, even family."[74] Buffy is shocked by the fact that Kendra sees slaying as the only important thing in life because, as Buffy argues, her friends and family are what make her such a strong fighter. The emotions and teen angst that Buffy brings to the table help her to be a strong slayer, even if they do distract her from this supernatural calling at times. In her struggle to reconcile her identity as an adolescent female and her destiny as the vampire slayer, Buffy constantly grapples with how to hold onto her normative teen qualities while being the most powerful vampire slayer in the history of slayers. This is one of the most complex struggles that Buffy must deal with, because she is trying to fulfill her role in both teen culture and vampire culture without being alienated from either world.

Essentially, the premise of *Buffy the Vampire Slayer* is that one girl has been chosen to save the world from dark powers. But underneath this storyline lies the life of Buffy Summers, a character who both rejects and embraces the cultural values of what it means to be a teen girl. While facing the Master, the most evil vampire in season one, Buffy says, "I may be dead, but I'm still pretty. Which is

---

73 *Buffy the Vampire Slayer*, Season 2, Episode 3.

74 *Buffy the Vampire Slayer*, Season 2, Episode 3.

more than I can say for you."[75] Buffy shows in this quote, and many others quite like it, that she is a teen girl who worries about her appearance, her relationships, and her place in the world. In her opening to the book, editor of *Ophelia Speaks: Adolescent Girls Write About Their Search for Self*, Sara Shandler describes her own struggle with seemingly superficial concerns about appearance that are often experienced by many teen girls. Shandler writes:

> Adolescence is not what I thought it would be. Happy endings aren't inserted conveniently before the last commercial break. The peer pressure isn't unrelenting, the wild parties aren't dangerously tempting, the first loves aren't thrillingly perfect. But, more unsettling than the unforeseen tedium, my face isn't blemish-proof and my stomach isn't immune to bloating.
>
> I was fed a cookie-cutter standard of beauty, and I do not invariably meet the media's image of perfect. As a media baby, I'm a disappointment.[76]

These concerns may seem quite superficial, but the average adolescent female is worried about the image that she projects to the rest of the world. In a subculture such as the world of teens, appearances are often everything and judgments about an individual's character and ability to belong to a certain group are determined by their outward appearance.

Buffy's supernatural abilities allow her to fulfill her calling as the slayer, but it is her normal teen characteristics that she shares in common with her scripted peers on the television screen and the teen audience. In Buffy's case, the supernatural elements of the show define her as an outsider, and they definitely complicate her participation in teen culture. But Buffy's teen girl qualities make her easily accessible to the teen audience at the same time: she has friends, romantic relationships and faces the typical constraints of high school life in academics and parental expectations.

---

75 *Buffy the Vampire Slayer*, Season 1, Episode 12.

76 Sara Shandler, *Ophelia Speaks: Adolescent Girls Write About Their Search for Self.* (New York: HarperCollins Publishers, Inc., 1999), 3.

Buffy's best friend, Willow Rosenberg, is one example of a social outsider who is able to participate in teen culture despite her unpopularity and association with the supernatural world. Buffy quickly befriends both Willow and Xander, even though Cordelia Chase (the popular girl at Sunnydale High) warns Buffy that Willow and Xander are not part of the "right crowd." Willow is portrayed in the first two seasons as Buffy's sidekick, the best friend of the slayer. Willow's friendship with Buffy allows her to experience the dual roles in teen culture and vampire culture, as Willow is often a part of the battles against evil forces in Sunnydale while still participating in everyday life at Sunnydale High School. In the second episode of season three, after Buffy has returned from Los Angeles, it is clear that Willow is hurt by the fact that Buffy deserted her and the life she was so connected to in Sunnydale. Willow says to Buffy:

> I mean, what about me? My life. I have all sorts of – I'm dating. I'm having serious dating with a werewolf, I've been studying witchcraft and killing vampires. I didn't have anyone to talk to about all this scary life stuff. And you were my best friend.[77]

Willow is hurt by Buffy's absence, because as Buffy's best friend, Willow has been there for Buffy through her own tough times and Willow expected the same in return. Willow begins to emerge as a character in her own right, one with "scary life stuff" to deal with, and supernatural powers all her own. As the series progresses, Willow becomes a more accepted member of teen culture as well as a force to be reckoned with in the supernatural fight of good versus evil.

Willow struggles with her own identity as an adolescent female, even while participating in the world of the vampire slayer. Her inexperience with romantic relationships is a common obstacle for many teens, and Willow must confront her insecurities and lack of confidence throughout the first few seasons of *Buffy*. In episode eight of the first season, Willow finds a nice boy online whom she wants to meet and start dating. Her vulnerability and desire for male attention in this episode is something that many teen girls can

77 *Buffy the Vampire Slayer*, Season 3, Episode 2.

relate to, especially adolescent females who do not have a lot of experience with the opposite sex. Unfortunately for Willow, this boy that she meets online is actually a demon trapped in the computer. Not only is this a cautionary tale about the dangers of online dating, but it sends a message regarding Willow's lack of experience with romantic relationships. The supernatural element here is not something that many teen girls would have experienced, but the emotions and feelings of not being wanted by boys in the shadow of the beautiful Buffy Summers is a storyline that many teen girls could relate to. Willow is insecure when it comes to negotiating a relationship with someone she is romantically interested in, while Buffy is bold and more experienced with dating. Willow is an important character on this series because she faces normative teen issues and addresses them in much different ways than Buffy. The two girls are both representatives of normal teen behavior, yet they are able to deal with situations and teen struggles with romance, family, and identity in completely different ways.

Xander Harris is a teen boy who is grappling with his own version of adolescent identity and struggles with romance, family, and friendships. Xander, Willow, and Buffy quickly become best friends in the first season, and Xander's character provides a male perspective on the adolescent angst of teen dramas. Xander's romantic feelings toward various females on this series is one of the most prominent topics for his character in many episodes. His girl-crazy status, his infatuation with Buffy, and his tormented relationship with Cordelia are central issues in Xander's high school life. His jealousy over Buffy's feelings for Angel become apparent in the first season, as Xander says to Buffy, "You're in love with a vampire? What, are you out of your mind?"[78] Later, in season three when Xander discovers that Buffy has been hiding a recently-returned-from-hell Angel, he is irate. Xander confronts Buffy about her secret, and it is obvious that he is both personally betrayed and also angry because Buffy has compromised the safety of those he cares about in order to have a relationship with Angel (once again). Buffy tries to explain, "I just wanted to wait." To which Xander replies, "For what? For Angel to go psycho again the next time you

78 *Buffy the Vampire Slayer*, Season 1, Episode 5.

give him a happy?"[79] Xander tries to be the protector of both Buffy and Willow throughout the series, especially when it comes to their romantic relationships. The importance of Xander Harris as a central surreal teen on *Buffy* is that although he is not a participant in the supernatural world to the extent that Buffy is, Xander does exist in both teen culture and vampire culture. As an adolescent male, Xander is often confronting normative teen issues of identity and romance, even while he is an active participant in the world of vampire slaying.

Xander's own romantic entanglements include a seduction by the substitute Biology teacher who turns out to be a giant bug that lures virginal boys to her nest, and a budding romance with an Incan mummy who sucks the life out of her victims to stay alive and keep her human appearance. Xander also falls hard for slayer Faith, but the most normative teen romance that Xander has in the first three seasons of *Buffy the Vampire Slayer* is his romance with Cordelia Chase. Cordelia and Xander are basically complete opposites, as Cordelia reigns over the popular crowd and is very involved in cheerleading and school activities. Xander, on the other hand, is part of the outsider crowd that only includes himself, Willow and Buffy. Despite their mutual dislike for one another at the beginning of the series, the physical attraction between these two teens is undeniable. Halfway through season two, Xander and Cordelia definitely fall for one another, a relationship that is kept secret for several episodes. They meet secretly, and although both try to resist their attraction for the other person, they are unable to keep their distance. Both fear that their friends will look at them differently because of their choice in romantic partners. Cordelia's desire to be accepted and adored by her peers is very strong, and although Xander does care about the opinions of his friends, he is not as easily affected by the thoughts of the popular crowd, because he has never been a part of it.

Peer acceptance and teen romance are intertwined in the relationship between Cordelia and Xander, because their feelings for

79 *Buffy the Vampire Slayer,* Season 3, Episode 7.

one another are often influenced by the opinion of their friends and schoolmates. This is a normative adolescent problem, because maintaining appearances and social acceptance are qualities that many teens seek. As David Elkind discusses in detail, the connection between appearing to belong to the teen culture and being accepted by one's peers is a critical aspect of the adolescent culture. Elkind writes, "Ownership of the icon identifies the adolescent belonging to a privileged group. And the sense of belonging is what fads are about. That is why the inability to possess the icon is so painful to those teenagers who must forgo it."[80] In keeping with this argument, Elkind goes on to point out that the need for peer acceptance is so strong in adolescence because many teens are trying to distance themselves from their dependence on family, and especially parents. Instead of searching for parental acceptance as children, teens are now seeking peer validation.

With each of the main characters at Sunnydale High, inclusion in the popular crowd (or at least an acceptable group if not the most popular clique) is either a desire or a requirement to continue in their role. Cordelia Chase is the stereotypical popular cheerleader, the queen of the high school who is spoiled by her parents and both loved and hated by her peers. After Cordelia finds Buffy talking with Willow and Xander (whom Cordelia views as extremely uncool outsiders prior to her romance with Xander), she says: "I don't mean to interrupt your downward mobility, but I just wanted to tell you that you won't be meeting Coach Foster – the woman with the chest hair – because gym was canceled due to the extreme dead guy in the locker."[81] As a resident of Sunnydale, where situations such as "extreme dead guys in lockers" are not that unusual, Cordelia takes much of the supernatural phenomena in stride. She is presented as too important to bother with the small issues, because her life and her status in teen culture are of utmost concern. Cordelia is concerned with her role in teen culture and fights to be the typical teen girl by participating in extracurricular activities at school, socializing with the popular teens, and keeping her outward

80 Elkind, 37.

81 *Buffy the Vampire Slayer*, Season 1, Episode 1.

appearance up to the standards set by her peers.

Cordelia Chase is a surreal teen character that resembles the teen girls whom many teen viewers may have encountered in their own high school experience. She is always brutally honest, even when the truth is quite obvious or will crush someone's feelings. Although it may seem that Cordelia is presented as nothing more than the pretty, shallow cheerleader, showcased by such lines as, "Great. Now I'm going to be stuck with serious thoughts all day,"[82] she is an integral part of the first three seasons of this series. Initially, she acts as the antithesis to the writers' desire for Buffy to be a strong, independent, capable adolescent female who is not completely consumed by being popular and beautiful. Yet, as the series goes on, Cordelia becomes a more well-rounded character who challenges Buffy, Willow and Xander in their roles and draws in reactions from viewers that the other main characters could not have ignited.

These four characters are the backbone of normative teen culture as presented by the adult creators of *Buffy the Vampire Slayer*; Cordelia the popular girl, Willow the insecure nerd, Xander the goofy outcast, and Buffy the pretty new girl with a mysterious secret. Each character is representative of a teen stereotype, and they all struggle with the same issues that Hersch and Elkind equate with a normal adolescence: the need for peer-group approval, displaying the right symbols of teen culture, and participating in normative teen behavior such as attending the high school Homecoming celebration and graduation. Their lives as seen in the storylines of the series are often influenced by other characters, such as Giles, Joyce, Angel, Faith, and Oz; but ultimately, it is Buffy, Willow, Xander and Cordelia that represent normative teen life. Their lives as surreal teens in the fictional town of Sunnydale, California are created by adults and the characters are often played by adult actors. However, it is important to remember that these adults have had their own experiences as teens that allow them to create realistic teen characters. The adult constructions of adolescent reality as seen through these central characters on *Buffy* do not alter the impact

82 *Buffy the Vampire Slayer*, Season 3, Episode 4.

of this show on its teen audience. Even though adults are behind the creation of these teen characters, the surreal teens on this series are able to capture many elements of normative teen behavior and participation in teen culture. Aside from the supernatural forces of vampires, demons, and witchcraft, the normal "life stuff" that each of these teens face are familiar situations for the teen audience of *Buffy the Vampire Slayer*.

Feeling Like an Alien in Roswell, New Mexico

Roswell explores many of the issues that normal teens face, as well as looking in detail at the individual identity quests of adolescents. The character analysis for this teen television series will focus on the three main alien-human hybrids and the girl who first discovers their secret identities. *Roswell*, like *Buffy the Vampire Slayer*, often focuses on the supernatural connections of its teen characters while at the same time presenting images of normative teen culture. As mentioned earlier, Patricia Hersch argues that oftentimes the dramatic and sensational stories about teens in today's world often overshadow the stories of normal teen behavior. However, the characters on *Roswell* are able to combine the two worlds of normal teen culture and the world of the supernatural. Neil Badmington discusses the complex relationships between the characters of *Roswell* in his essay, "*Roswell High, Alien Chic and the In/Human*":

> 'Complicated', I think, is the perfect word to describe the intricate series of connections that *Roswell High*[83] traces between its human characters. Love and friendship are seen to lie at the heart of everyday teenage life, affecting how people connect, disconnect and reconnect with each other. And these connections are as strange as they are complicated.[84]

The characters that bring these complicated storylines of normative teens and supernatural chosen ones to life are human teen Liz Parker, and alien-human hybrid teens Max Evans, Isabel Evans,

83 *Roswell* is called *Roswell High* in England.

84 Neil Badmington, *Roswell High, Alien Chic and the In/Human*." *Teen TV: Genre, Consumption, Identity*. Edited by Glyn Davis and Kay Dickinson. (London: British Film Institute, 2004), 171.

and Michael Guerin.

Liz Parker is the most "normal" central adolescent character on *Roswell*, because unlike Max, Isabel, and Michael, she does not have any supernatural powers or status as a half-alien. She is a teen girl with a plan for the future. That is, until Max Evans heals her and causes her to question the most basic truths in her life. As Liz thinks aloud in the third episode, "The future was always so clear to me. A straight path towards my goal. I just never counted on there being intersections."[85] Liz Parker is a "normal teen girl" dealing with everyday issues that most teens face: dating, school, family, part-time work. She participates in high school activities and excels in academics, and struggles with questions of her own identity as well as the importance of her relationship with her parents and friends. However, when Liz begins to have a friendship with Max, she sees that there are possibilities in the world that she never considered before. Liz sees a whole new world open up to Max because of his alien side, and she is intrigued by the thought of a world outside of her small-town life in Roswell, New Mexico.

Liz is perhaps one of the most self-aware teens on the three series under analysis here. Although less self-absorbed than the famously self-analytical teens on *Dawson's Creek*, Liz is extremely introspective, and her thoughts are often captured by the writers through journal entries and voice-overs at the beginning of many episodes. I believe that the writers have chosen to make Liz a thoughtful, self-aware adolescent female because this is a normative teen quality that many adolescent girls can relate to. During the teenage years, adolescents often question not only their place in the world, but their ability to participate in the normative aspects of teen culture. The thoughtful nature of Liz's character opens up possibilities for this teen girl to actually tell the audience what she is thinking, instead of leaving it open for interpretation as is often the case with teen television dramas.

At the same time, Liz is very concerned with the well-being of her friends and family, and is loyal to the point of sacrificing her own heart's desires for the good of Max. For instance, in season three,

---

85 *Roswell*, Season 1, Episode 3.

"Future Max" visits Liz and tells her that if she does not give Max up, it will cause the end of the world in the future.[86] At first not believing Max from the future, Liz is skeptical but she soon agrees to make Max believe that she does not love him. She even goes to the extreme of asking Kyle (her ex-boyfriend) to come over to her house and pretend to be in bed with her, as if they are involved in a sexual relationship. Liz plans this so that Max will see her with Kyle and assume that they have gotten back together – thus, guaranteeing that Max will fall out of love with Liz. This is one example of Liz's strength being demonstrated by self-sacrifice, a theme that will be repeated throughout the series.

Unlike Buffy Summers, Liz Parker is not chosen to save the world, nor is she specifically selected by fate to fight evil. While Buffy is fighting demons, Liz is trying to protect her boyfriend's secret identity. Yet, there are many similarities in the powerful female role that each character fills. Liz's role is much more in line with the traditional female calling to protect one's family and friends, but that does not make it any less purposeful. Liz does not hesitate to fight for the people that she loves, as seen in "The White Room" episode from season one where Liz, Michael, Isabel, Maria, Tess and Alex plot to save Max from the government alien-hunters who have captured him in their classified facility. Liz drives Max to safety as the group splits up in the next episode, "Destiny," and the government agents follow them. As Liz and Max are on the run together, she tells him, "We choose our own destinies, remember?"[87] Yet, when forced to make the decision that will ultimately affect not only Max, Michael, Isabel, and Tess (the alien-human hybrids on Earth), but also their entire species on their home planet, Liz chooses to let Max go. Liz's devotion to Max is so great that she is able to give him up in order for him to fulfill his destiny. Liz is able to combine the traditional mission of women as protectors of their homes and families with the strength and courage of a young woman with self-confidence and an awareness of her potential to make a difference in the lives of others. She is by no means a weak or less capable female teen character because her strength lies in self-sacrifice instead of

86 *Roswell*, Season 2, Episode 5.

87 *Roswell*, Season 1, Episode 22.

supernatural powers.

The viewers are able to see a strong sense of self-worth and a positive self-image in Liz Parker. She makes choices that display her own security with who she is, because Liz's worth is found within herself, and she is clear about the person she wants to be, and the values that she will not compromise. Even as her attraction to Max intensifies, Liz is still capable of making her own decisions and following her intuition instead of allowing a relationship with someone else to control her. Sometimes adolescent females lose their own identity once they become involved in a romantic relationship. The need to please someone else becomes stronger than the desire to make one's self happy. In her discussion of the struggles of adolescent females when it comes to romantic relationships, Mary Pipher, M.D. turns to Simone de Beauvoir. Pipher writes:

> Simone de Beauvoir believed adolescence is when girls realize that men have the power and that their only power comes from consenting to become submissive adored objects. They do not suffer from the penis envy Freud postulated, but from power envy...Adolescent girls experience a conflict between their autonomous selves and their need to be feminine, between their status as human beings and their vocation as females. De Beauvoir says, 'Girls stop being and start seeming.[88]

In contrast to this argument is Liz Parker, who remains autonomous and self-sufficient even after her romance with Max begins. Liz's normative teen qualities and her strength as a female teen allow her to be a strong teen character on *Roswell.*

Max Evans is the chosen leader of the teens on *Roswell*, and he is on a mission to save his beings on the alien planet he has never known, and also to preserve the relationships that have been established on Earth with his adoptive parents, Liz, and his friends. In season three, Michael begins to resent the fact that Max is the chosen leader. In "Who Died and Made You King?", Michael becomes the leader when Max dies (an odd similarity between Buffy

88 Mary Pipher, *Reviving Ophelia: Saving the Selves of Adolescent Girls.* (New York:Ballantine Books, 1994) xiii.

and Max in that they both die for just a moment), but Max quickly takes the power back. His role as the king of his home planet calls for him to be the leader among his alien-human hybrid peers as well. Liz supports Max in many of his decisions, but she does not let his supernatural role define who she is. His role as the leader is directly linked to Liz's role as the protector of Max's secret and the self-sacrifice that characterizes Liz's connection to the supernatural world. Max has chosen Liz, and she in turn, chooses to help him and support him. Her role is no less important, and it is crucial to recognize that Liz has chosen (not been subjugated to) a particular role in order to exist in this supernatural world.

At the end of season one, Max's adoptive parents begin to have suspicions about his behavior. This suspicion will intensify as the series continues, culminating in his parents' discovery of who Max and Isabel really are. However, in season two it seems that the Evans' solution to Max's turmoil is therapy. As the psychologist tells Max that his problems are normal and something that many teens experience, Max thinks to himself, "Well, I guess the natural place to start is that I'm an alien. A hybrid, actually. You know, human DNA mixed with alien DNA, that kind of thing."[89] While many teens feel that they are ostracized by dominant culture, Max's genetic makeup as half-alien-half-human complicates his identity even more. Throughout the series, Max is constantly trying to hide his identity from someone, whether it is Sheriff Valenti in season one, or the residents of Roswell, New Mexico in season two, or his parents in season three. This struggle leaves Max vulnerable to scrutiny, and he is always trying to prove that he is a capable leader. Many adolescents can identify with this search for identity, because it is a common experience of everyday teens. Max's questions about his own identity are a result of his participation in teen culture and supernatural alien culture. The physical intimacy that Max shares with both Liz and Tess throughout the series is presented in a way that allows the audience to see the vulnerability of Max as an insecure teen, a normative teen concern. Max and Liz experience visions and intense attraction towards one another throughout the series. Because of Max's relationship with her, Liz begins to see the future in the third season. "This is getting really weird,

89 *Roswell*, Season 2, Episode 1.

Max."[90] Liz is worried that her relationship with Max is getting a bit too alien for her, but Max reassures Liz that things will turn out fine, even though he himself has never experienced this emotional, spiritual, and physical connection before. This is another example of normative teen behavior, as the pressure of becoming physically intimate with someone (both social pressure from peers and physical pressure from one's own hormones) affect many teens involved in romantic relationships.

In the case of Tess, Max learns that he is meant to be with her in their alien reality, but he resists this until his relationship with Liz has fallen apart in season two. Max turns to Tess for comfort, and they have sex, an event that Max discusses with his best friend, Michael.

> Michael: You and Tess actually had…
> Max: Hot alien sex. Yes.
> Michael: How was it?
> Max: Well, it's probably a lot like human sex.[91]

Max's connection to Tess does not end with the physical intimacy of sex because their bond is now sealed with Tess having conceived a baby. In keeping with their alien side, the baby grows rapidly. Although this is not the typical teen pregnancy storyline on television dramas of this time period, *Roswell* attempts to tackle teen issues by putting the alien spin on it. The time escalated nature of alien pregnancy allows for a heightened explanation of teen pregnancy on this series as a real teen issue, as the urgency of the situation is increased due to the fact that the baby cannot survive on Earth. Decisions must be made quickly, and lives are altered in a matter of days as news of Tess's pregnancy makes its way from one character to the next. This storyline also highlights the fact that many teens experience life-altering situations regardless of how much of an outsider each individual teen may feel like at one point or another.

The third focal character on *Roswell* is Isabel Evans, the twin sister of Max and second member of the Royal Four, a term used to describe Max, Isabel, Michael and Tess since they were all royalty

90 *Roswell*, Season 2, Episode 16.

91 *Roswell*, Season 2, Episode 19.

in their alien reality. Isabel Evans is very much a sought-after girl at Roswell High. As Liz points out to her in the first season, many of her peers view Isabel as someone with supermodel-status beauty. Yet, she is also quite intimidating, especially in the eyes of Liz's human best friend, Maria DeLuca. In season one, Isabel basically uses her powers to tease Maria once she learns of Isabel's secret identity. For instance, in episode two, Isabel and Maria are stuck in Maria's car together since Isabel's car has broken down. Isabel knows that Maria is very uneasy about the alien-human hybrids, and their supernatural powers. The two girls have the following verbal exchange:

> Maria: Does your mother know?
> Isabel: What, that she does stupid things?
> Maria: No, that you and Max are...you know, different...
> Isabel: You mean horrible disgusting creatures from outer space who sneak into your room at night and per form excruciating experiments?[92]

Maria has a horrified look on her face, and suddenly crashes into the back of Sheriff Valenti's car. Meanwhile, Isabel sits back rather calmly and seems to enjoy Maria's discomfort in this situation. Isabel puts on a very tough front, in an effort to hide her own insecurities. In keeping with normal teen girls, Isabel often feels insecure, even if she does not reveal these insecurities to her peers.

In a majority of the episodes, Isabel is much more content than Max and Michael to lead a normal human life. After Isabel learns that Max has shared their secret identity with Liz, Isabel says to him, "I can't believe this Max. You know, I finally feel like I have a quasi-normal existence and you go and blow it all with one random act of lunacy."[93] She is upset by the notion that this will disrupt her life in Roswell. Isabel wishes to participate in the activities that most teen characters experience as a part of their normal lives. During the holiday season, Isabel is nicknamed "The Christmas Nazi" by her family and friends because of her intense need for everything to be perfect. In season two's "Roswell Christmas" epi-

92 *Roswell*, Season 1, Eposode 2.

93 *Roswell*, Season 1, Episode 1.

sode, she chastises Max for not picking out the right Christmas tree. Isabel inspires Max to heal all of the sick children in the hospital, as "Calling on Angels" is playing in the background. As Lynn Schofield Clark describes in her book *From Angels to Aliens*, the need to guard ourselves and others against unexplained tragedies such as the shootings at Columbine High School and the national tragedy of September 11, 2001 is often seen among teens as well as adults. Schofield Clark describes, "We don't always consciously seek explanations for terrible events that occur in our lives. We want things that will help us guard against evil, things that offer protection and support…"[94] This adolescent idealism, in wishing to heal all social and physical problems in the world, is something that many teens hope to obtain as they seek out spiritual identities for themselves. Isabel is searching for a way to control the normal aspects of her teen life, and she views Christmas as a way to do that and keep the unknown from ruining her participation in normative teen culture.

The final central character on *Roswell* is Michael Guerin, who is also an alien-human hybrid and member of the Royal Four. As soon as Michael learns that there may have been other aliens on their ship when it crashed, he searches desperately for any link he can find to his other reality. Michael's participation in normal teen culture is limited by his unfavorable home life, but he does succeed in breaking free from his abusive foster parent when he becomes legally emancipated. Although Michael attempts to exist on his own, associating only with Max and Isabel at the start of the show, he becomes romantically involved with Maria and begins to embrace his life as not only a half-alien, but as a half-human teen. Michael and Maria have a fairly combative relationship, and they are constantly bickering with one another. Gradually, Michael is able to be honest with Maria about his insecurities and his fears about his own identity. Finally, at the end of season two, Michael and Maria have sex for the first time and tell each other "I love you." Their emotional bond is even more evident when Michael decides that he cannot leave Earth, because he finally has a life as a normal teen in Roswell, which is what he has been searching for since the crash.

The teen characters on *Roswell* are most definitely surreal teens,

94 Clark, 27.

because they are representative characters of normative teen behaviors that real teens are able to recognize. As Neil Badmington points out in his essay on *Roswell*,

> Teenagers, it seems, would not be teenagers if they did not act a little inhuman, a little alien-ated, from time to time. The inhuman (alien) passes for human (teenager) by appearing inhuman (alien-ated truant), and the traditional opposition between the real and the simulated finds itself even deeper in crisis.[95]

One of the most basic shared characteristics of teens in America is the feeling of alienation that many experience. As Badmington argues, teenagers are often set apart from dominant culture, so it is only reasonable that they would act accordingly at times. On *Roswell*, the teen characters are presented as more than human in an attempt to draw parallels between that which is normal and that which is alien. The alien qualities of these teens are additive, and do not make them less human than real teens. *Roswell* combines the two as teen aliens are half-human and half-"not of this world." In combining the normative qualities of these teen characters with the supernatural, it becomes more clear that teens exist in both dominant culture (often as outsiders) and within the subculture of teens. Interestingly enough, even the human teens are alienated from the dominant adult culture.

A Messenger of God – Joan of Arcadia

Just as Buffy and Liz have been chosen to exist in the supernatural world, Joan Girardi has been selected by God to carry out specific tasks, even as she exists in normative teen culture. It seems that many of the duties God asks Joan to perform are within the realm of "her world" - the teen reality that she is familiar with and, many times, among the people that she knows. Before the handsome young man first claiming to be God approaches Joan on the street, her life is not out of the ordinary. Joan lives with her parents and her two brothers, and they have recently moved to Arcadia

95 Badmington, 169.

where Mr. Girardi has taken a job as the new chief of police. Joan is a teenage girl searching for her own identity while coping with the everyday challenges of many teen girls, from arguments with parents to getting in trouble with teachers at school to crushes on teen boys.

Joan's secret identity as the messenger of God begins to complicate her life as a normal teen girl. Since Joan is usually a very forthright person, her parents become suspicious when she is not open with them about her life once God comes to Joan with her first mission. From this point forward, Joan becomes more secretive as she must keep quiet about the fact that she is carrying out God's instructions. If people were to find out that she is having conversations with God, and even more that she was performing tasks at God's request, they might begin to wonder if she is sane. Because of her newfound reluctance to participate in family discussions or offer any information about what is going on in her own life, her parents' initial reaction is that Joan is hiding information that could put her in danger. When Joan's father, Will, questions her about this sudden secrecy, Joan responds, "Dad, it's called high school. Everyone's hiding something."[96] Joan's participation in teen culture is marked here by her language, as she bluntly dismisses her father's concern.

In this same episode, Joan is shocked to discover that one of the most popular cheerleaders is responsible for disposing of her infant in a trash dumpster, a case that Police Chief Girardi is working on. Although this is not a situation that all teen girls face, teen pregnancy and the subsequent baby-dumping is something that had become more common (or at least brought out in the open much more according to the media) in the early 2000s. *Joan of Arcadia* often tackles this type of real life issue in a different way than *Buffy* or *Roswell*. Instead of focusing solely on the impact of these life issues on the teen characters, *Joan of Arcadia* presents the issue from both the teen viewpoint and the parental perspective. *Joan of Arcadia* describes this situation in a serious manner, even having Joan's father discuss the newborn's mother and the other options that she had, such as leaving the baby at a hospital or other "safe place" according to California law.

96 *Joan of Arcadia*, Season 1, Episode 6.

The dumping of a newborn baby in a dumpster leaves students at Arcadia High wondering who is responsible. Once it is discovered that the cheerleading captain, Brianna, is responsible for the "disturbing dumpster baby news"[97] as one cheerleader calls it, Joan is nervous about the treatment she will receive from the other cheerleaders since it was Joan's mother who turned Brianna into the authorities. Luke makes a flippant reference to anorexia in his suggestion that the cheerleaders will not attack Joan because they probably do not eat much anyway.

> Luke: You think they know?
> Joan: What, that Mom turned in their alpha dog? Probably. They're going to eat me alive.
> Luke: I wouldn't worry. Probably anorexic, or at least vegetarian.[98]

This casual reference to anorexia shows how familiar this eating disorder is among teens, both in the early 2000s and present-day. As Mary Pipher argues, "Anorexia is both the result of and a protest against the cultural rule that young women must be beautiful. In the beginning, a young woman strives to be thin and beautiful, but after a time, anorexia takes on a life of its own."[99] The cultural reality is that, according to the National Eating Disorders Association, "Anorexia nervosa typically appears in early to mid-adolescence" and "between 0.5 and 1% of all American women suffer from anorexia nervosa."[100] Although Luke's comment to his sister is meant to cheer her up and make her less nervous, it also shows that eating disorders are a problem for real teen girls within American culture. Unfortunately, issues with eating disorders, self-mutilation, and other self-destructive behaviors have become common in normative teen culture over the last several decades as we see these scenarios play out on the screen far too often.

The "Bringeth It On" episode is significant to this study because it captures many of the teen stereotypes that are associated with

---

97 Ibid.

98 *Joan of Arcadia*, Season 1, Episode 6.

99 Pipher, 204.

100 National Eating Disorders Association, 2002. www.edap.org

normal teen culture. As Michael Bamberger describes in his ethnography of one American high school in Pennsylvania in the early 2000s, there are certain types of normal teens at most American high schools. Bamberger writes, "The roles must be filled. A high school must have politicians, athletes, beauties, scholars, musicians, poets, actors, clowns, insiders, outsiders, and large numbers of the unexceptional."[101] These are the characters in normative teen culture, including the "unexceptional" teens who live their lives largely unnoticed by their peers or teachers. In this pivotal episode of *Joan of Arcadia*, the characters of normative teen culture are brought into the spotlight. The real life issue of teen pregnancy creates quite a stir at Arcadia High School, and brings the various members of teen culture together in a common goal as they search for the truth behind this unexplained tragedy.

As a central teen character on the show, Luke Girardi has a hard time in high school as peer pressure to be cool and parental expectations to be "normal" weigh heavily on him. In fact, Luke questions, "Do you sometimes wonder if high school will ever come to an end?"[102] Luke takes academics extremely seriously, which is in stark contrast to his sister, Joan. Basically, Luke is your average, awkward teen male who is struggling with questions of identity, insecurities with females, and pressure to be a certain type of strong male (not unlike Xander Harris or Kyle Valenti from *Buffy* and *Roswell* respectively).

Luke has a bit of a crush on Grace Polk, the bad girl whose sexual preferences are a joke among the popular cheerleaders at school. As many so-called outsiders can confirm, any sign of someone who rejects the markers of normative teen culture in high school as far as behavior, dress, or extracurricular activities is often targeted for ridicule by the popular kids. Grace and Luke both belong to this group of outsiders, but it appears that they did not socialize much before Joan and Grace became friends. Luke struggles with expressing his feelings for Grace, and their romance is one of the most subtle and least physically explicit of the romances on the three television series in this study.

101 Michael Bamberger, *Wonderland: A Year in the Life of an American High School* (New York: Grove Press, 2004), 5.

102 *Joan of Arcadia*, Season 1, Episode 11.

Finally, the friendships that Joan has with Adam and Grace are basically her saving grace throughout the first season. Unfortunately, her friendship with Adam is broken midway through this season, because Joan follow's God's orders to destroy Adam's artwork in order to keep him from dropping out of school to pursue art as a career. Joan's intentions are not malicious, but Adam takes this attack on his art very personally (and understandably so). Even with this huge stumbling block in their relationship, the feelings between Adam and Joan become more romantic as the first season of the series continues. In fact, it is Adam that Joan finally confides in, as she suffers from Lyme disease in the hospital in the final episode of season one. Adam supports Joan even though he may not believe that she actually hears from God. Instead of basing their relationship solely on physical attraction, they have formed a romantic relationship built on friendship with a solid foundation of trust that allows Adam to believe Joan.

Adam Rove is an artistic young man who exists on the fringes of the teen culture at Arcadia High School. Adam is an extremely introspective person, and he does not share his emotions or thoughts very often in this series. Instead, his feelings about love and relationships come out when he is faced with a truly thought-provoking situation. Such is the case when Joan tells Adam that a little boy whom she babysat, named Rocky, has passed away. Adam remarks, "Rocky died. Wow. Life sincerely sucks."[103] Language is a cultural marker of teens, and the abrupt yet concise view of Adam here is representative of the different ways in which teens are distinguishable from dominant culture. Instead of being offended by his short remarks regarding the death of someone she cared about, Joan understands that Adam is being sympathetic even though his words make it appear that he is not concerned or impacted by the situation. Joan and Adam are both participants in normative teen culture, so they have an understanding of each other's language, whereas an adult might take Adam's comment to be less than sincere. The simplicity of dialogue here captures a key element of real teen culture, in that verbal expression is not always as articulate or drawn-out as one might see on teen dramas such as *Dawson's Creek*

103 *Joan of Arcadia*, Season 1, Episode 12.

or *One Tree Hill*. Adam conveys exactly what he is feeling with these six words, and *Joan of Arcadia* reveals a realistic conversation among two teens who are grieving.

Grace Polk is the final central teen character of *Joan of Arcadia*, and she is also a representative of normative teen culture, even though she is often not accepted by her peers. Grace is content to be her own person, and I believe that she is one of the teen characters with the most security in her own identity. In expression of her unique identity, she dresses in a traditionally labeled "masculine" manner, from her baggy pants and T-shirts to her leather jacket. Because of her resistance to cultural demands for teen girls to dress a certain way (short skirts, midriff-baring tops, and tight jeans), Grace is often targeted by the cheerleaders and other peers for her "manly" appearance, and is labeled as a lesbian. Grace does not appear to be influenced by the elements of consumer culture that appeal to many teens. Instead, Grace marks herself as unique through her dress, language, and resistance to high school peer pressure. Although Grace is painfully aware of the rumors about her sexuality, she does not seem to let them control her. In fact, she takes the initiative and kisses Luke at the school dance. This is an act of bravery, and one of defiance as her peers watch her dispel the rumors about her sexual preferences. This act can also be seen as a reinforcement of cultural demands for hetero-normality, as sexual identities during the teen years become very important as markers of normalcy or deviance.

One common element between *Buffy*, *Roswell*, and *Joan of Arcadia* in terms of the normative teen behavior of the central characters is the female friendships. These friendships help to sustain a sense of normalcy for the focal female teen characters. As discussed, Buffy's friendship with Willow and Liz's friendship with Maria help Buffy and Liz to have a stable relationship with someone whom they completely trust in spite of their supernatural circumstances. These friendships allow real teens to relate to the characters because of the connections that can be drawn between the friendships on the screen, and those in real life. Although Joan and Grace's friendship does not appear to be as rock solid from the beginning, it becomes more clear as the first season progresses that this is an important friendship to both Joan and Grace. They rely on one another and are loyal and protective of each other. Granted, there are instances of betrayal as Joan must join the cheerleading squad at God's request, which Grace views as Joan turning her back on their friendship. Even then, Grace expresses concern for Joan because this decision is completely out of character. The fact that Joan is able to have stable relationships with both Adam and Grace stands as a testament to her role in normative teen culture.

The connection between normative teen culture and the spiritual callings of Buffy, Joan and Liz in the supernatural world results in each of these female characters filling dual roles. Through their supernatural callings, these teen characters are able to enact adult roles while still facing the normative teen issues of identity questions, friendships, and romantic entanglements. These standardized teen issues anchor the characters in adolescent culture, while their otherworldly obligations allow them to engage in fulfilling a higher purpose outside of their regular teen existence. The identity and spiritual quests of these three young women are central to the development of each teen television series under analysis here. Buffy, Liz, and Joan directly interact with and are influenced by the rest of the teen characters on *Buffy, Roswell,* and *Joan of Arcadia,* but it is now time to shift the focus to the individual quests of these three surreal teen girls.

Jenn Burton

Chapter 8

Wait, Who Are We? Identity Quests of Buffy, Liz & Joan

Throughout her study of America's adolescents, published in 1998, Patricia Hersch argues that today's teens have been set apart from dominant culture and are left feeling alienated and alone. Hersch contends that teens are "a tribe apart" because their everyday experiences are unlike the lives of their adult counterparts. She writes, "Adolescence is rife with drugs, alcohol, cigarettes, sex, lying, violence, unstable and broken families, and so on. This is the mainstream of adolescence today."[104] Hersch highlights the identity quests of real teens, as a normative experience of teen culture. An identity quest is most easily described as discovering one's own identity and sense of purpose. As Lynn Schofield Clark describes, "Identity is understood as the way in which we adopt certain strategies of action to maintain a connection with others, with our past, and with our own aspirations."[105] Thus, an identity quest is a search for the formation of an identity that will allow individuals to make connections with others, with the past, and with personal goals and a purpose in life. As seen in Hersch's analysis of teens in America today, the everyday trials and tribulations of life as a teenager are challenging enough without added pressures of existing in both teen culture and the supernatural world.

---

104 Hersch, 366.

105 Clark, 11.

On *Buffy the Vampire Slayer*, *Roswell*, and *Joan of Arcadia* the audience sees focal female teen characters who have the benefit of supernatural powers to endure the trials they face, yet they are also confronted with complicated situations brought on by their roles within a larger supernatural realm. Buffy Summers, Liz Parker, and Joan Girardi are each fulfilling roles that have been chosen for them. These roles call for each female teen to play a special part in the spiritual or supernatural world, yet they are still forced to navigate normative teen issues of friendships, family conflicts, and romantic relationships. These girl warriors have each been chosen for a specific purpose and called to fight for a certain cause, yet they are still teen girls seeking to understand and answer questions of their own autonomy and identity. Their spiritual roles complicate the identity quests of Buffy, Liz, and Joan as each one searches for her place in teen culture and the larger spiritual realm to which they each belong. Where the previous chapter has examined the normative, day-to-day experiences of teens, this chapter will focus on the purposefulness of identity as the supernatural calling of each of these chosen characters is explored.

One Girl in All the World: Buffy Summers

> You know, I just wanted to start over, be like everyone else, have some friends, you know, maybe a dog. But, no. You had to come here. You couldn't go suck on some other town.[106]

When Buffy Summers arrives on the scene at Sunnydale High School, she is attempting to leave her former life as the vampire slayer behind. According to *Buffy the Vampire Slayer* lore, there have been slayers since the beginning of time, dating back to the earliest days of man. As the audience will learn in later seasons, the slayer was created by using evil and combining it with the strength to fight that evil. Although the history of the slayer is somewhat complicated, and the pieces to this puzzle are not put together until much later, it is clear from the very first season that the slayer is a transhistorical figure that has been chosen to fight evil. Buffy is again confronted with her calling as the vampire slayer when she

106 *Buffy the Vampire Slayer*, Season 1, Episode 1.

meets the school librarian, who is actually her official watcher. The watcher is in charge of looking after the vampire slayer, and he is also chosen for this specific purpose. Buffy's watcher is a British gentleman posing as the high school librarian, Mr. Giles. He has to have a cover story so that they can keep Buffy's identity as the slayer secret.

In the first episode of the series, Buffy is definitely trying to abandon her role as the vampire slayer and leave it behind in Los Angeles when she moves to Sunnydale. She faced problems at her previous high school, mostly due to her duties as the slayer. The new principal at Sunnydale High School questions Buffy regarding her sordid past.

> Mr. Flutie: You burned down the gym.
> Buffy: I did, I really did, but…You're not seeing the big picture here, I mean, that gym was full of vamp… asbestos.[107]

Buffy has come to the small town of Sunnydale because of her mother's new job opportunity at an art gallery in town. She plans to forget about her calling as the slayer, and live her life as a "normal" teen girl. Unfortunately for Buffy, Rupert Giles has also been sent to Sunnydale to ensure that she fulfills her role as the slayer.

> Giles: A, a Slayer slays, a Watcher…
> Buffy: …watches?
> Giles: Yes. No! He, he trains her, he, he, he prepares her…
> Buffy: Prepares me for what? For getting kicked out of school? For losing all of my friends? For having to spend all of my time fighting for my life and never getting to tell anyone because I might endanger them? Go ahead! Prepare me.[108]

Buffy's life has been completely turned upside down because of her calling as the vampire slayer, and the first season of the series is a reflection of her adjustment to her role in the supernatural world of good and evil.

---

107 *Buffy the Vampire Slayer*, Season 1, Episode 1.

108 *Buffy the Vampire Slayer*, Season 1, Episode 1.

The powerful words that frame the opening images of *Buffy* in the series montage throughout the first season tell the story of the slayer. "In every generation there is a Chosen One. She alone will stand against the vampires, the demons, and the forces of darkness. She is the Slayer."[109] These words are critical to understanding what exactly it means for Buffy to be the vampire slayer. "In every generation there is a Chosen One" indicates that the slayer is a transhistorical figure, as one is chosen in each generation of people. The fact that there is "One" slayer is also important, a key point that will be toyed with on *Buffy* after she dies in a battle with the Master, but is brought back to life by Xander. Once Buffy has died, a new slayer is called; so beginning in the second season, there are actually two slayers which goes against the historical precedence of a "Chosen One" – making Buffy an outsider even in her set apartness as the slayer.

The next words in this powerfully repeated statement sets the tone for this series: "She alone will stand against the vampires, the demons, and the forces of darkness." In many instances, Buffy is destined to fight alone, even though she has a support system of friends that want to help her. In the end, it is Buffy who has to destroy the evil forces that exist in Sunnydale. Buffy knows that she will ultimately be the one who has to fight this battle against evil and the forces of darkness for the rest of her life, and she repeatedly tells Willow, Xander, Giles and Angel, "I can handle this" and "this is my fight."[110] Her relationships with family and friends make her a stronger fighter because she wants to protect the people she loves from evil in the world – but Buffy knows that she has been chosen and, therefore, she must be willing and able to fight alone and stand on her own two feet. Her calling has pushed her to become more autonomous than she might have been without her duties as the vampire slayer. She must be independent, capable of making her own decisions, and willing to act based on those choices. If she fails at autonomy, Buffy will also fail at being the vampire slayer.

Finally, it is these qualities of the historical importance of the slayer, as well as the autonomous nature of the vampire slayer that

109 *Buffy the Vampire Slayer*, Season 1, Episode 11.

110 *Buffy the Vampire Slayer*, Season 2, Episode 1.

combine to set Buffy Summers apart from her peers. As the opening words say, "She is the Slayer" – the one girl chosen in all the world to fight vampires, demons, and the forces of darkness. According to this declaration, Buffy Summers is defined by her role as the vampire slayer. Yet, the series also focuses on her identity as a teen girl. How are these two roles reconciled and how does Buffy Summers simultaneously exist in the world of teen culture and the world of vampires and demons? According to cultural critic and cultural studies professor, Lynn Schofield Clark, many real teens engage in a quest for spiritual meaning and a feeling of purposefulness in the world. In this search for meaning and attempting to merge the worlds of teen consumer culture and individual autonomy, many teens struggle with their own identities. Clark writes, "Identity construction is an ongoing process guided by the need each of us have to consciously make sense of our choices, and the often unconscious ways in which these choices create a form of social solidarity with (or distinction from) others."[111] Buffy has been spurred on to a spiritual quest by her calling as the "Chosen One." As Buffy struggles to understand why she has been chosen as the slayer, she must also confront everyday issues of life as a teen girl. Yet, as Jenny Bavidge explains in her essay on teen heroines in the media, "Buffy's Slayer identity distances her from the other 'destinies' of girlhood she might otherwise have adopted."[112] Does this mean that in her spiritual quest as the Chosen One, Buffy has disregarded the normative roles of a teenage girl? In many ways across the series, Buffy must do just that, yet at the same time, she does not want to completely remove herself from teen culture. Buffy's spiritual quest helps to define who she is and the roles that she will play in society, but Buffy does not let her calling as the vampire slayer completely dominate her life. She continues to take part in the teen culture that surrounds her at Sunnydale High School, leaving Buffy with two (often oppositional) roles as a teen girl participating in adolescent culture and as the vampire slayer existing in the supernatural world.

Buffy is extremely resistant to her calling when she first arrives in Sunnydale, but once her watcher Giles confronts her with the

111 Clark, 11.

112 Bavidge in *Teen TV*, 48.

duties that she must perform, Buffy begins to accept her identity as the vampire slayer. When Giles brings out the transhistorical *Vampyr* text (in which Buffy's destiny is written) in the first episode of the series, Buffy automatically backs away in a physical enactment of refusal to fulfill her calling. Later, after discovering that the dead body of a teenage boy has been found at the high school, Buffy and Giles again discuss her destiny.

> Giles: You think it's coincidence, you're being here? That boy was just the beginning.
> Buffy: Why can't you people just leave me alone?
> Giles: Because you are the slayer. Into each generation, a slayer is born. One girl in all the world…
> Buffy: …Blah, blah, blah. Been there, done that. I'm moving on.[113]

Try though she might, Buffy is ultimately unable to refuse her role as the vampire slayer because it is her spiritual fate to fight evil. Although she again tries to resist her duties when she runs away to Los Angeles at the end of season two, Buffy never strays from her slayer duties for too long. She returns to Sunnydale and resumes her role as the slayer, because she cannot allow the demons, vampires, and forces of darkness to control the world. Plus, her slayer work followed her to Los Angeles anyway, so she was unable to avoid her calling even in a new city. Spiritual questing is a struggle that many individuals have faced. In many instances, religion or a religious calling has filled the void and helped to make clear the unexplained evil in the world. As Schofield Clark points out in *From Angels to Aliens*, "Religious practices thus have some talismanlike functions. We hold onto them both as a means to solidify our connection with the good and with God, and to distance ourselves from the inexplicably bad."[114] Buffy's supernatural role allows her to play out the spiritual questing of adolescence, bringing religious faith and perspectives on good and evil onto the teen television stage. Buffy slays vampires as a way of fulfilling her role as a warrior fighting

---

113 *Buffy the Vampire Slayer*, Season 1, Episode 1.

114 Clark, 27.

on the side of good in the supernatural battle of good versus evil. Beyond that, Buffy's slaying is also a way of finding purpose in her identity and addressing the adolescent need to have some element of control in her life. Buffy might not be able to control how her boyfriend feels about her or if she is accepted by her peers, but she can always triumph over the demons and vampires.

Spiritual questing is described by Lynn Schofield Clark in her work on teens and the supernatural in the media. According to Clark, "the interest in the supernatural is related to increasing concerns about evil throughout the last decade of the twentieth century and the beginning of the twenty-first."[115] Because of this renewed interest in the supernatural and spiritual realm as a result of cultural uneasiness about unexplained evil, teen viewers can use supernatural teen television series as an outlet for their spiritual questions. Clark argues that shows such as *Buffy* and Buffy's spin-off show *Angel* were significant in their approach to the spiritual world.

> These programs were also groundbreaking in the way that they reintroduced otherworldly enemies into popular fictional television after a several-decade hiatus. In this way, they also did something else: they told stories of a spiritual battle between good and evil with an almost complete disinterest in organized religion.[116]

Buffy's journey as the vampire slayer is one that calls her to be the protector of her classmates, family and friends. As the spiritual quest and search for identity involved in being both the vampire slayer and a teen girl influence Buffy's life, the audience is also able to see Buffy as a girl warrior. She fights to protect those that she loves, and the home and life she has built for herself in Sunnydale. The most vivid example of Buffy as a protector is seen in the Prom episode from season three, which is Buffy's senior year of high school. As the class spokesman, Jonathon gives the senior class awards for "Class Clown" and "Most Likely to Succeed", and begins to discuss the weird occurrences at Sunnydale High.

115 Clark, 26.

116 Clark, 47.

> Jonathon: Whenever there was a problem or something creepy happened, you seemed to show up and stop it. Most of the people here have been saved by you or helped by you at one time or another. We're proud to say that the Class of '99 has the lowest mortality rate of any graduating class in Sunnydale history. And we know at least part of that is because of you. So the senior class offers its thanks and gives you this. It's from all of us. And it has written here – Buffy Summers…Class Protector.[117]

Buffy makes her way to the stage, shocked by the gratitude of her peers, and accepts the trophy from Jonathon. Risking her life many times to save the residents of Sunnydale from evil creatures has culminated in this shining time for her. In this one moment in her life, all of the sacrifices that Buffy has made in order to exist in both vampire slayer culture and teen culture are worth it. Interestingly, Buffy comes to this realization at her Senior Prom, when she is about to graduate from high school. As the center of teen culture, high school has been the locus of Buffy's desire to participate in normative teen girl activities. Finally, someone has recognized the wonderful gift that she has given by fulfilling her spiritual role as the vampire slayer, even as she was often forced to sacrifice certain normal teen activities to do so.

The questions that many adolescents face regarding their own identity and who they want to be in the world often leave individuals feeling lost and confused. As Sara Shandler says in her introduction to *Ophelia Speaks*: "We are all aware that we have been raised in a culture that cradles double standards, impossible ideals of beauty, and asks us to listen. But we are caught in the crossfire between where we have been told we should be and where we really are. Self-directed girls are sometimes lost."[118]

Buffy, as a girl warrior, is not a lost girl because her role as the vampire slayer gives her purpose outside of normative teen culture. As Shandler discusses in 1999 during the same time as *Buffy's*

117 *Buffy the Vampire Slayer*, Season 3, Episode 20.

118 Shandler, xii.

popularity, many teen girls experience an identity crisis because of the cultural demands of what teens should be and the everyday struggles that teens must endure. The lost girls are not only those whom Peggy Orenstein describes in *Schoolgirls: Young Women, Self-Esteem, and the Confidence Gap* as "girls who become pregnant, girls who join gangs, girls who marry young and leave school are often said to have 'fallen through the cracks.'"[119] The lost girls also include average female teens who are struggling with their identity and searching for who they want to be in the future.

Buffy Summers goes through an identity exploration as an adolescent female throughout the first three seasons of *Buffy the Vampire Slayer*. Like many adolescent females, Buffy is trying to deal with questions regarding her own identity, even as she copes with her duties as the slayer. Buffy's search for self is complicated by her spiritual calling, but she grapples with the same overarching inquiries as most teenagers during this time period.

> Buffy: Nothing's ever simple anymore. I'm constantly trying to work it out – who to love, or hate, who to trust. It's just like the more I know, the more confused I get.
> Giles: I believe that's called growing up.
> Buffy: I'd like to stop then, ok?[120]

The formation of an identity is a crucial part of growing up, and Buffy wishes to refuse this process even though in reality, growing up cannot be stopped. The identity formation that takes place during adolescence is often confusing and challenging for many teens. As David Elkind points out, "modern writers described adolescence as a period of storm and stress, of emotional turmoil and conflict. The late Erik Erikson, the last of the preeminent advocates of modern adolescence, described the period as one during which the adolescent's task was to construct a sense of personal identity."[121] Buffy is both biologically destined and supernaturally called to become a

---

119 Peggy Orenstein, *Schoolgirls: Young Women, Self-Esteem, and the Confidence Gap* (New York: Anchor Books, 1995), 199.

120 *Buffy the Vampire Slayer*, Season 2, Episode 7.

121 Elkind, 15.

strong young woman, and she cannot refuse either role as she embarks on her identity quest.

Many scholars who have examined *Buffy* as a cultural artifact see evidence of Buffy Summers as a feminist character because Buffy is portrayed as an independent, strong, self-directed female. After looking closely at the first three seasons of *Buffy the Vampire Slayer*, it is clear that certain conclusions could be drawn regarding Buffy as a feminist character. In commonplace definition, a feminist is "a person whose beliefs and behavior are based on the belief in the social, political, and economic equality of the sexes."[122] However, professor and feminist writer Imelda Whelehan gives a more specific definition of feminism in *Modern Feminist Thought: From the Second Wave to 'Post-Feminism'*. Whelehan writes, "All feminist positions are founded upon the belief that women suffer from systematic social injustices because of their sex and therefore, any feminist is, at the very minimum, committed to some form of reappraisal of the position of women in society."[123] Buffy, then, is a television character who has been written to believe in feminism and equality for men and women, as evidenced by her words and behavior throughout the series.

The fact that the vampire slayer is a female indicates that the writers of this show have respect for the power of females, and the important role that all women should play in society. For example, in the third season, a new watcher comes to town and tries to boss Buffy around. In the following dialogue between Wesley (the new watcher) and Buffy, she displays her assertiveness and unwillingness to take orders from anyone, also showcasing her snarkiness.

> Wesley: Are you not used to taking orders?
> Buffy: Whenever Giles sends me out on a mission he always says please. And afterwards I get a cookie.[124]

---

122 www.dictionary.com

123 Imelda Whelehan, *Modern Feminist Thought: From the Second Wave to 'Post-Feminism'*. (New York: University Press, 1995), 25.

124 *Buffy the Vampire Slayer*, Season 3, Episode 14.

Earlier in the series, Buffy must fight Angelus (Angel's evil vampire alter-ego) in order to stop the world from ending. As they fight to the death, Angel tries to verbally intimidate Buffy, but she is strong and knows that she is capable of winning this battle.

> Angelus: Now that's everything, huh? No weapons…no friends…no hope.Take all that away…and what's left?
> Buffy: Me.[125]

Buffy is not only a teen heroine fighting to save the world, but she is also a feminist character who is confident in her strengths and demands to be treated as an equal. Even though scholars such as Gwyneth Bodger have argued against Buffy as a feminist character, claiming that she is merely a pawn in the patriarchal system of slayers under the thumb of the Watcher's Council[126], Buffy's resistance to the cultural expectation for teen girls to be weak and in need of male protection define her as a feminist character.

As Jenny Bavidge discusses in her essay specifically focused on Buffy Summers as a teen heroine, the female hero can be traced back to "the mythic and historical tradition of disruptive women warrior hero at the same time that it beckons us forward…"[127] Thus, Buffy can be read as not only a strong feminist character of the 20th century, but also as a nod to the historic days of powerful woman warriors. Buffy is a powerful teen heroine, and there are definitely characteristics that she possesses that are indicative of a feminist character as well.

The characterization of Buffy Summers is one of the best representations of both independence and feminism within the teen television genre of the 1990s. Buffy's search for self and her influence on the lives of those around her are both central issues in this series. The spiritual and identity quests that Buffy takes up are a direct consequence of her existence in two worlds – adolescent

125 *Buffy the Vampire Slayer*, Season 2, Episode 22.

126 Gwyneth Bodger, "Buffy the Feminist Slayer? Constructions of Femininity in Buffy the Vampire Slayer." *Refractory: a Journal of Entertainment Media*, March, Vol. 2, 2003. www.slayage.tv

127 Bavidge in *Teen TV*, 41.

culture and the supernatural world of vampires and good versus evil. Buffy is both a feminist character and a teen heroine which influences her quests throughout the series.

An Alien Among Us: Liz Parker on Roswell

"The bigger your world gets, the bigger your problems get too."[128] In the words of Roswell's central female character, Liz Parker, expanding one's horizons and allowing new people and new ideas into one's frame of reference often leads to more complicated issues. At the beginning of the first episode of Roswell, Liz Parker is a teen girl working in her parents' restaurant and joking around with her best friend, Maria. Yet, that all changes in the blink of an eye when Liz is shot, and Max Evans magically removes a bullet from her abdomen. From this point forward, Liz is forever changed by the influence of Max's healing powers. For Liz, spiritual questing on Roswell involves her search for the place that she should occupy in the world, as well as the reason why Max chose to reveal his long-held secret to her. The alien-human teen characters on this television series – Max, Isabel, and Michael – are aware that their genetic makeup is a combination of human DNA and alien genetic material, but they do not know what this means in the larger sense of their futures and their role in two distinct worlds. As the alien-human hybrid characters embark on a literal search for self as they try to discover what exactly they are, Liz is engaged in her own questing.

The spiritual quest of Liz Parker is not a result of being called by higher powers to perform a specific duty, as is the case with the female lead characters on Buffy and Joan of Arcadia. Instead, Liz is trying to discover who she is and how she has been changed as a result of Max healing her. This becomes both an identity quest and a mystical journey as Liz follows Max on various adventures to unearth the secrets of his identity and confront the supernatural elements that have now become a part of both of their lives. From the moment Max saves Liz, they are constantly fighting to stay together despite the expressed destiny of Max to be with Tess, his young

128 *Roswell*, Season 1, Episode 5.

bride from their alien reality. At the end of season one, Liz chooses to walk away from Max in an attempt to give him the opportunity to fulfill his destiny as leader of the Royal Four. Although painful, this action is indicative of self-sacrifice by Liz Parker that is not seen in many other teen television dramas. In contrast to Buffy and Joan, Liz does not possess any supernatural powers, but she is chosen to exist in the supernatural world of the alien-human hybrids. The self-sacrifice that Liz displays throughout the series in giving up her own desires for the good of others, connects Liz to Buffy and Joan in that they are all called to participate in a supernatural world. Liz's sense of identity and intention to discover her own place in the world, with or without Max Evans, is extremely strong and she will continue to build this already powerful sense of who she is throughout the three seasons of this show.

Lynn Schofield Clark views Buffy and Angel as powerful television series in part because of their presentation of the supernatural and the spiritual as an explanation of spiritual battling not necessarily linked to organized religion or Christianity. Similarly, Roswell approaches the battle between good and evil in an entirely innovative way, beginning with the character of Liz Parker. Liz is made spiritually powerful through her physical and emotional connection to Max Evans. She is chosen by him to protect the knowledge of his secret identity, much like Buffy Summers chooses friends and family with whom to share her hidden identity as the slayer. Yet, on Buffy the good guys are easily distinguished from the bad guys: evil is physically marked with vampire fangs, distorted faces, and other demon characteristics. On Roswell, the audience is kept guessing as to whether or not Max, Michael, and Isabel are the good guys or the bad – they are the unknown "other" whom normal teens such as Liz Parker are taught to fear. Yet, the positive aims of the alien-human hybrid teens challenge the traditional views of the unknown as bad or frightening. Instead of the alien-human hybrids being the bad guys, the evil characters of Roswell's first season are human government agents who torture Max in the final episode of this season.

This new way of presenting good and evil, with the evil (mostly adult) characters disguised as normal humans and the good (mostly teen) characters hiding their secret alien identities, sets Roswell apart in spiritual questing on teen television dramas. Alien identities on this series become a way of expressing teen alienation and a search for a way to serve a purpose in the world. For Max and Isabel, feeling alien is something that truly frightens them. In the first season, when Tess arrives in Roswell, both Max and Isabel experience feelings unfamiliar to them.

> Isabel: Did you feel like something inside of you is changing, like waking up?
> Max: Something primal…
> Isabel: Instinctive…
> Max: Something not human…[129]

Although these alien feelings are frightening for Max and Isabel, they have felt alienated from many of their peers because of their secret identities. The experience of feeling as though they do not belong is not new to them, but they continue on their quest to discover their own identities: both alien and human.

Roswell presents this new way of looking at good and evil in keeping with the theme of teen idealism versus adult corruption. As mentioned previously, wish fulfillment of teens to be part of something bigger than themselves is often in contrast to the reality of normative teen life. On *Roswell*, the reality is that adults are often corrupt and uncaring about the lives of others, while the teen characters are self-sacrificing and searching for their identity in the context of how their role in the world will affect others.

For real teens who experience a sense of alienation or feeling as though they do not belong, their participation in normative teen culture becomes limited and oftentimes painful as they are ostracized from the group. For Monica, a fifteen-year-old client of psychologist, Dr. Mary Pipher, this feeling of alienation as experienced

129 *Roswell*, Season 1, Episode 19.

by Max, Michael and Isabel on *Roswell* is a similar situation to Monica's own sense of not belonging. Pipher writes,

> Monica had more perspective on her problems than most girls her age, but unfortunately, insight does not take away pain. She told me ruefully that she hated her fat body and hence, herself...She said, "Let's face it, the world isn't exactly waiting for girls like me." She'd resisted the culture's definitions of what was valuable in girls, but she was tired. She said, "When I walk down the halls I feel like a hideous monster. I understand my parents' point that looks aren't that important in adulthood, but I'm not in adulthood."[130]

Monica is alienated from her peers because of her appearance, and the alien-human hybrid teens on *Roswell* are alienated because of the need to protect their secret identities. Just as an alien identity, E.T., was used to critique normative earthly practices in 1982, the half-alien existence here literally identifies idealistic teens as "alien." On *Roswell*, these alienated members of teen culture are the good guys, and they represent the feelings of alienation experienced by many normative teens.

The character of Liz Parker is also evidence of a fresh approach to questions regarding identity and spirituality within the teen television drama genre. Where Buffy and Joan have been chosen to lead in their supernatural realms, Liz is selected by Max to protect his secret identity. Liz is the link between aliens and humans on *Roswell*, and she is called to fulfill a role of self-sacrifice and protection of her alien-human hybrid friends. When Liz asks Max why he risked his life to save hers, he simply tells her "because it was you."[131] Liz and Max's relationship undeniably affects her decisions throughout the series, but it is equally clear that Liz has a sense of who she is as a human being, and the fact that she is a strong female teen. In this passage from season one, Liz is thinking about how much her world has changed. The reference to Marie Curie shows that Liz is

130 Pipher, 170.

131 *Roswell*, Season 1, Episode 22.

someone who is seeking to pursue her own educational goals and that she admires women who were pioneers in their field of study. Liz thinks aloud:

> Here were my plans for last night – finish my shift, dinner with the parents, then a half hour of talking with Maria on the phone, then dive into this issue I have with Geometry, and hopefully finish in time to watch this A&E biography on Marie Curie. Instead, I took off in an open-aired vehicle that probably shouldn't be allowed on the road to begin with, broke into a house, essentially stole things from it, and engaged in general bonding with aliens. Welcome to my world.[132]

Liz is coping with the ways her life has changed since becoming involved in the supernatural world of Max, Isabel, and Michael. Her normative teen desires of wanting to talk on the phone with her best friend, eat dinner with her parents, and watch a television program focusing on the life of a woman she admires are all captured in this passage. At the same time, her role in the supernatural world has also been highlighted by Liz's thoughts here. She is a strong female teen who is able to exist in both teen culture and alien culture, much like Buffy and Joan both exist in two worlds.

In conversations with Maria and in her own private thoughts, Liz is often wondering whether her relationship with Max has changed who she is. During season two, Liz comes to the realization that she needs to break off her relationship with Max because it has started to take over who she is as a person. As a strong female, Liz is not willing to let herself become lost because of her romance with Max. Liz says to Max:

> I just re-read *Romeo and Juliet*, and you know the first thing that I realized is that isn't even the title. It's called *The Tragedy of Romeo and Juliet*. They die. You know she's this young girl. She…she's younger than me and she dies. Look, I think the reason why people think that it's such a romantic play is they don't know what it's like to be put in that position. But

132 *Roswell*, Season 1, Episode 7.

> when your life, and other people's lives are put at risk there isn't anything romantic about it. Max, you can't stop what is happening to you. I mean your life will always be dangerous. But my life…it doesn't have to be. My life is only in danger if I am with you. I want to be in love with boys. Normal boys. I want to see my 21st birthday. I want to have a wedding day. I want to have children, and I want my children to be safe. You know Max, if…just if you truly love me you'll let me go. I may love you, but I don't want to die for you. [133]
>
> This scene captures Liz's assertiveness and her unwillingness to lose her own identity for any reason, even if her relationship with Max must end because of it. Liz is a normative teen girl with a sense of social and personal responsibility – she wants to help others and she also does not want to give up who she is as an individual.

Adolescent relationships are often extremely complicated, but Liz does not even realize the obstacles that are about to be brought into her life once she becomes close to Max. In a world where teen girls are often finding themselves lost in their adolescent romances, Liz Parker is a strong female who displays autonomy in her decision-making and a strong belief in herself. Just as Buffy is capable of making her own choices and following through on her instincts in battle, Liz is able to make her own decisions and carry out actions that she believes to be in the best interest of herself and those she cares about. An example of this is when Liz gives Max up in the final episode of season one.

> Liz: So everything Nasedo told me was true. You and Tess were meant to be together.
> Max: Liz.
> Liz: I mean, it's your destiny, right?
> Max: I wish I could go back Liz. Back to when things were normal.
> Liz: Me, too. I just wish that I could have stopped you from saving my life that day in the CrashDown. [134]

133 *Roswell,* Season 2, Episode 18.

134 *Roswell,* Season 1, Episode 22.

Liz recognizes that it is Max's destiny (according to the alien reality) to be with Tess. In an arguably selfless move, Liz leaves Max with Michael, Isabel, and Tess in the pod chamber where the four alien-human hybrid teens were born. Many teen girls would not be willing to sacrifice their teen romance for the good of both people involved, but Liz takes a powerful step forward in her journey towards autonomy. She follows her instincts and rests assured that although her decision brings pain, it will also provide the best future for both her and Max even if they are not together.

Liz Parker definitely displays certain characteristics involved in feminist thought. In the late 20th and early 21st centuries, it is not unusual to see feminist characters on the television screen. Conversations between Liz and Maria show that each girl is trying to be self-confident, strong, and independent despite the questions that each have about the future.

> Maria: I don't know. I don't know. Which one is better for me? You can see the future, Liz, please tell me. Hold my hand, maybe you'll have a flash or something. Tell me which one is better?
> Liz: Maria. Maria, listen to me, you've got to stop, okay? Who knows, all right? I can see the future, and I have no idea. Maybe you just need to decide what you want and then go get it. Okay?[135]

Even as the alien-human hybrid teens as well as the normative teen characters are in danger of being killed, Liz is able to remind Maria that she needs to make the best decisions for herself. As journalist Gloria Steinem states in the introduction of *To Be Real: Telling the Truth and Changing the Face of Feminism*, "The greatest gift we can give one another is the power to make a choice. The power to choose is even more important than the choices we make."[136] In the case of Liz Parker, viewers might write her off as a teen girl caught up in the emotions and weaknesses of romantic love and

---

135 *Roswell*, Season 3, Episode 18.

136 Rebecca Walker, ed. *To Be Real: Telling the Truth and Changing the Face of Feminism* (New York: Anchor Books, 1995), xxvi.

adolescence. However, the writers of the show obviously wanted to portray Liz as a strong female character, one that believes in equality of the sexes, and equality among humans and alien-human hybrids (or cultural others). As Gloria Steinem points out, the power to choose for one's self is a critical aspect of feminism. Liz Parker – in choosing to participate in Max's supernatural world and also choosing at certain points to walk away from her romance because staying would mean giving up her own identity – shows that she is a feminist character.

In *Roswell* as in *Buffy*, feminist ideology is integrated into the quest for autonomy in the scripting of Buffy Summers and Liz Parker. In defining feminism as a belief in re-evaluating the position of women in society and displaying qualities of assertiveness and self-awareness that are indicative of a belief in women's equality, Liz Parker can be identified as a feminist character seeking autonomy as she embarks on an identity quest. As Clark points out, "we need to recognize that television programs and films are polysemic: that is, they are open to many levels of interpretation, from the obvious and literal to the metaphorical and mythical."[137] As cultural texts, these teen television series are all open to the interpretation of cultural critics – whether that may be *Buffy* or *Roswell* media scholars or the fifteen-year-old teen girl watching each show on the television screen. As a teen character, Liz Parker occupies a space in both the teen culture reality in which she actively participates, and the supernatural realm into which she is introduced because of her connection to Max Evans. Her spiritual and identity quests are evidence of Liz's strong sense of herself as an individual person capable of making her own decisions and playing a part in each of these worlds.

A Messenger of God: Joan of Arcadia

The first episode of Joan of Arcadia begins with a scene of sixteen-year-old Joan Girardi tearing through her clothes, trying to find the right outfit to wear to school that day. She catches a glimpse of a man lurking outside her bedroom window, and runs downstairs

137 Clark, 47

to tell her parents and her two brothers. No one believes her, and Joan goes off to school a bit disturbed that her family seems unaffected by the fact that she saw a man outside her window. On the way to school, Joan is confronted by an attractive young man, who claims to be the same guy that she saw earlier that morning outside of her bedroom window. He then shocks her by stating that he is God. Joan is in disbelief and is also uneasy about how much this man seems to know about herself and her family.

> Joan: Hey, God. Get lost, I mean it.
> God: I know you think you mean it.
> Joan: You know, I'm going to give my father a full description and a composite drawing of you before dark.
> God: Well, maybe he'll be too busy thinking of creative ways to ground you for nodding off in French class.
> Joan: Are you spying on me?
> God: I'm omniscient, Joan. It comes with the job.[138]

Joan is very hesitant to believe that God has chosen her, but she goes along with it. Her first mission is to apply for a job at the Village Book Store, which ultimately convinces her older brother, Kevin, to move on with his life and stop dwelling on the fact that he is now paraplegic. Even after Joan carries out the first mission asked of her by God (who appears as many different people in her daily life, from the cute stranger to a cafeteria worker at her high school to a punk goth teen), she is still unsure about whether or not this is God whom she is having conversations with on a regular basis. As an adolescent, Joan is trying to find her place in the world, and this newfound spiritual journey that she is being sent on simply adds more confusion to her identity quest.

Joan Girardi is the central female character on *Joan of Arcadia*, and her identity quest as a teen girl is the focal point of many episodes. Adolescence is a time when many people struggle with questions of who they are and who they want to be. For Joan, this struggle to define herself is complicated by spiritual questions as a result of God's appearance in her life.

---

138 *Joan of Arcadia*, Season 1, Episode 1.

Joan: Who are you?
God: I've known you since before you were born, Joan.
Joan: I'm going to ask you one more time.
God: I'm God.
Joan: You're what?
God: God.
Joan: Don't ever…talk to me again.[139]

Obviously, Joan does not believe that God would show up and choose her to speak to or carry out his missions on Earth. According to the storyline of this series, Joan promised God that she would change a lot of her behaviors if only he would let her older brother, Kevin, live after his horrific car accident. God reminds her of these promises, and Joan begins to think that maybe this person is who he says he is, because he could not have known about those promises otherwise. Joan's own religious beliefs are not strong, and her faith is constantly wavering. Her family is not particularly religious, so she does not understand why she has been chosen by God.

Joan: I'm not religious, you know.
God: It's not about religion, Joan. It's about fulfilling your nature.[140]

Joan's spiritual calling by God requires her to follow his "suggestions" in order to impact the lives of people in her town. For example, in episode four of season one, God asks Joan to have a garage sale. When she is sorting through her family's belongings to find items for the sale, Joan discovers a painting of her mother's and this pushes her mother to start working on her art again. Later, in episode eight of this season, Joan destroys Adam's sculpture because God asks her to prevent it from being exhibited. Although this act destroys Joan's friendship with Adam for several episodes, God has asked Joan to prevent Adam's work from being shown because Adam is considering dropping out of school in order to work on his art full-time. Although the adolescent discovery of self which

139 *Joan of Arcadia*, Season 1, Episode 1.

140 *Joan of Arcadia*, Season 1, Episode 1.

is encouraged by Adam's artistic abilities is important, it does not exclude the need to complete his education. In order to exist in teen culture within dominant culture, teens must balance self-discovery with social expectations. For Adam and Joan, this need to fulfill societal expectations nearly ruins their relationship. Thus, Joan has been called by God to carry out specific duties on Earth in order to positively impact the lives of those around her, even if the mission might seem odd or extremely unbeneficial to everyone at the time. Joan's spiritual journey as a result of God's influence on her life is definitely a crucial part of her own understanding of identity and the supernatural world.

Joan Girardi is presented on *Joan of Arcadia* as a stubborn, sometimes selfish, and often contemplative teen girl. Her life is undeniably impacted by her family, and the presence of family ties and friendships throughout the first season of this series is incredibly strong. In the first episode, Joan's mother asks Kevin to speak to his little sister because she is worried that Joan is having a hard time.

> Helen (Joan's mother): When your sister gets home, I want you to talk to her.
> Kevin: About what?
> Helen: She's going through something?
> Kevin: You think she's cracking up?
> Helen: No! I think she's going through something, and she needs a big brother. That hasn't changed.[141]

Whereas Buffy's parents and Liz's parents do not notice that each girl is dealing with new issues because of their supernatural destinies (even to the point that Buffy's mother does not ask about her blood-stained clothes or curious injuries, and Liz's parents seem to be oblivious to her overnight road trips with Max), Joan's family is very concerned about her well-being. This support system of friends and family has instilled in Joan a strong sense of who she is, and this allows her to seek her independence in a way that would be more unavailable to her without these strong family ties and friendships.

141 *Joan of Arcadia*, Season 1, Episode 1.

Coming of Age

Just as Buffy Summers and Liz Parker display characteristics in keeping with feminist thought, Joan is also a strong, independent teen girl who exhibits qualities in line with feminism. Joan displays her belief in the equality of the sexes in her behavior at school and at home. Also, Joan's mother, Helen, is an independent woman with a rewarding job outside of the home and an equally, if not more, rewarding job at home as a wife and mother. In "The Fire and the Wood" episode from season one, Helen begins a conversation at the dinner table, asking the whole family to participate. When she senses that her family is in trouble, Helen often initiates a way to solve the problem. She is a very involved mother to Joan, Luke, and Kevin. Helen's husband, Will, is also an involved parent and together they appear to have a very equal relationship. Thus, Helen acts as a strong female role model for Joan.

Like Buffy and Liz, Joan is a feminist character with a strong sense of her own independence and identity. Joan's family support, her positive role models, and her own sense of self-worth all add to her sense of identity. As Elkind states:

> An integrated sense of identity, as we have seen, means bringing together into a working whole a set of attitudes, values, and habits that can serve both self and society. The attainment of such a sense of identity is accompanied by a feeling of self-esteem, of liking and respecting oneself, and of being liked and respected by others.[142]

Interestingly enough, on *Joan of Arcadia* obvious references to feminist thought are few and far between. This indicates that feminism is assumed on this television drama, because there is no effort made to explicitly state that Helen, Joan, and Grace are feminist characters. Many quips are made that challenge the cultural model of femininity described in *The Feminine Mystique*, such as the following example from "Vanity, Thy Name is Human." Joan says to Grace, "We're both about more than superficial appearances. Like you!"[143] Also, the show's writers also seem to lean towards feminism

142 Elkind, 196.

143 *Joan of Arcadia*, Season 1, Episode 21.

in that they choose men and women to be God, although this may conflict with common traditions of portraying God as male at all times.[144] And, these same writers and producers of this series have chosen a female character to carry out God's missions. Feminism is an issue for teen girls in the real world as well, as shown by the following contribution in Sara Shandler's book, *Ophelia Speaks*. Sixteen-year-old Emma Christine Black writes,

> I argue when a friend falls powerlessly into the grasp of any guy who will hold her, then whimpers that he never asks her permission anymore and she can't get out of it. I fight to convince her that vulnerability is not a female requirement, but my best friend cuts designs into her arms with a razor blade because she finds herself unattractive. I watch my friends fall to sex, drugs, alcohol, their parents' wishes, their friends' wishes, suicide. I battle those who tell me, "You can't because you're a woman," and their only explanation is, "It's a hard world, that's just the way it is."[145]

For many teen girls, the feminist characters on teen television shows such as *Joan of Arcadia* are role models for how young women today can be assertive, independent feminists while still participating in normative teen culture and fulfilling their destinies.

Although Joan is not a religious person, she is a spiritual individual who has been selected to play a role in the supernatural world at God's request. She is also a participant in teen culture at Arcadia High School. This dual lifestyle that Joan must lead as she keeps her spiritual role hidden from the rest of the world makes her identity quest more difficult because she has also personal and cultural expectations to meet. God's requests of Joan often leave her alienated from other participants in teen culture. Just as Buffy and Liz struggle with living in teen culture and the supernatural world, Joan must exist in both the real world of normative teen issues and the spiritual world as chosen by God to perform certain duties.

The teen girl warriors seen on *Buffy the Vampire Slayer, Roswell,*

144 Examples of female representatives of God on *Joan of Arcadia* are the cafeteria worker at Joan's high school, and a little girl on the playground at the park.

145 Emma Christine Black. "Saving Sarah." Shandler, 276.

and *Joan of Arcadia* have each been chosen to fulfill a specific purpose in the supernatural world. Whether Buffy is slaying vampires in the Sunnydale graveyard or Liz is running from secret government agent alien-hunters or Joan is joining the cheerleading squad to discover which teen girl at Arcadia High School has dumped her newborn in a trash can, these young women are constantly searching for their place in the worlds that they occupy. Each of them must live a dual existence – one life in teen culture and one life in the supernatural world to which they have been called to play a part.

In contrast to Liz Parker from *Roswell*, Joan is chosen by a higher power to fulfill supernatural missions in the real world. Much like Buffy Summers, Joan is a player in the battle between good and evil, hand-picked by God to serve as a warrior. Even though Liz Parker stands out as someone who is not specifically chosen by a higher power such as fate or God, all three females – Buffy, Liz, and Joan – are called to join in the fight between good and evil. Their roles are all very different, as Buffy physically fights demons and vampires, Liz protects the secret identities of her boyfriend and friends, and Joan follows instructions given to her directly by God to have an impact on the everyday lives of people around her. Yet, they are all strong teen girls who live in two distinct worlds – the world of teen culture and the world of the supernatural.

The religious narratives found on shows such as *Buffy*, *Roswell*, and *Joan of Arcadia* offer a new perspective on the impact of autonomy and the search for identity in light of the spiritual experiences of these characters. According to Clark, "religious narratives of identity may include stories of direct personal experiences with a Sacred Other, as well as practices that are 'recognized as religious' because they have been handed down through a religious tradition that recognizes transcendence."[146] These personal narratives can be seen in the lives of characters such as Joan Girardi, Buffy Summers, and Liz Parker. These spiritual roles help each character form a strong sense of who she is, which leads to the creation of identity and a sense of belonging in the world.

146 Clark, 11.

The ability to transcend or connect to a larger supernatural "other" gives Buffy, Liz, and Joan a clear self-perspective. For example, Buffy knows that she is capable of beating Angelus without weapons, friends, or help of any kind. Her calling as the slayer has made her a strong teen girl, and her sense of identity and self-worth give her more confidence. Liz Parker is able to see the future, and in the final few episodes of season three, she is the one who makes the decision to allow Tess to live even though Tess murdered Alex. Liz knows that even though she is part of the supernatural world, she is still a teen girl who could not live with the weight of deciding whether someone lives or dies. Also at the end of this season, Liz begins getting visions of the death of herself and her friends. Instead of panicking, she reacts by making a decision for herself to leave Roswell with Max after high school graduation. Finally, Joan, like Buffy, is quite resistant to her calling at first. After carrying out many missions that God has asked her to perform, Joan becomes more confident in who she is as a person because she is filling a role in the supernatural world that she has specifically been chosen for. Unfortunately, season one ends with Joan questioning whether or not her communication with God has been real or a side effect of the Lyme disease that has infected her body. Until the final episode of season one, Joan is secure with her place in normative teen culture because she has a sense of belonging with her friends and boyfriend. Joan is also more confident in her role as a spiritually chosen individual, and she is more accepting of the requests made of her by God. All three central female characters are able to achieve self-confidence, perspective on their place in the world, and a sense of independence in part because of their connection to the supernatural world.

That each of these television series focuses on a strong female character in one way or another speaks for the cultural shift in attitudes towards autonomy and feminism, explored in the context of the adolescent search for identity. Previously, the teen years have been viewed, and therefore presented in the media, as wasted years. As Donna Gaines argues in her ethnography focusing on a group of teens in Bergenfield, New Jersey, "in reality, it was adult organization of young people's social reality over the last few hundred years that had *created* this miserable situation: one's youth as wasted years. Being wasted and getting wasted."[147] Yet, the females presented on these three series are anything but wasted youth. Buffy, Liz, and Joan are definitely set apart from other teens because of their supernatural callings, but they are also participants in normative teen culture. They each fulfill a purpose in the supernatural world, and their callings give their lives meaning.

---

147 Donna Gaines, *Teenage Wasteland: Suburbia's Dead End Kids*. (Chicago: University of Chicago Press, 1990), 86.

Chapter 9

Audience Responses

Buffy Summers, Liz Parker, and Joan Girardi allow the adolescent audience to imagine their lives as something bigger. The spiritual and supernatural roles of these characters do complicate the relationship between the characters of the show and the real teen audience, as a result of the dual roles they play. The dual roles seen in both groups connect the real teens to fictive teens even though they may not relate on the supernatural level. Real teens often endure their own spiritual and identity quests which are not unlike the supernatural quests that each of these fictive teens pursues. The supernatural elements on these TV shows may not be entirely realistic, but the presence of a supernatural "other" brings the issue of teen alienation to the forefront.

The link between normative teen issues presented by the teen characters on *Buffy*, *Roswell*, and *Joan of Arcadia* and the real teens can be found in audience response to each of the shows. Real teens who are participating in teen culture and are members of the teen audience for one or more of these television series provide the basis for further interpretation of these series as cultural texts. As Lynn Schofield Clark explains in the late 1990s, the lives of teenagers have become more complicated as concerns regarding teen pregnancy, abuse of drugs and alcohol, and teen hate crimes push many parents to encourage their teens to spend more time at home. Clark writes, "In this context, home-based media, including television, personal computers with Internet access, video games, 'home theater,' and stereo systems become an important yet not completely unproblematic alternative for young people's leisure time."[148] Now, the isolation created by the COVID-19 pandemic in 2020 has created an environment of heightened separation from peers, as most teenagers communicate through social media platforms, video conference calls, and texts rather than in-person. Their social activities no longer include the normative experiences of going to high school football games, meeting up at the mall, or going to the local fast food restaurant to eat together. The majority of adolescents today are experiencing life behind a screen for a good portion of their teenage years.

Because of this shift in the late 20th century to home-based activities such as watching television and playing video games, the role of the teen audience has become a multimedia experience. Not only are teens watching the television series, but they are also going online and discussing the shows with their peers. This network of technology has led to some audience response information for this study being found on the Internet on fan websites, discussion boards, and product reviews in the early 2000s. Also, audience response surveys were distributed among a select group of undergraduate students at California State University, Fullerton and personal acquaintances who were viewers of one or more of these television series. The surveys were distributed between June 2006 and September 2006 and the participants will be identified by first name only throughout this study.

First, the fan websites that will be used in this discussion of audience response were selected on the basis of quality of information pertaining to this study, as well as accessibility. Since all three of these television shows have been canceled or otherwise ended by the time of this writing, many fan websites have been eliminated from the Internet or are no longer maintained by the website creators and/or hosts. Along with specific fan websites,

148 Clark, 14.

the Internet also offers fan feedback on sites such as Amazon.com and TV.com. Considering the potential problems with online audience response information such as accountability of the fans posting information and the anonymous nature of the Internet, it is also important to note that audience responses for each of these teen television dramas were conducted with people in the "real" world outside of cyberspace.

I distributed audience response surveys in three undergraduate courses at California State University, Fullerton in the beginning of the fall semester of 2006. These classes were selected on the basis of targeting individuals who would have been teenagers at the time these television series aired, as well as my own familiarity with the American Studies department at CSUF. The surveys were distributed in American Studies 442: Television and American Culture, American Studies 401T: American Suburban Culture, and American Studies 350: Theory and Methods. Willing participants were given roughly two weeks to complete and return the surveys.

Along with distributing these surveys among undergraduate college students, I also contacted friends and acquaintances using social media networks in an open call for participation. In turn, some of these friends forwarded the information to people that they knew to be teen viewers of these television series. In approaching the audience response portion of this study by searching for a qualitative body of responses instead of a large quantity of responses, I hoped to collect teen fan reactions to *Buffy*, *Roswell*, and *Joan of Arcadia* that would display thoughtful reflection on these cultural texts. Also, since the audience response is only one aspect of this study of specific teen television dramas, this method of collecting audience responses proved to be the most effective and timely approach.

The audience for each of these series, like the entire subculture of teens, cannot be categorized or stereotyped by specific qualities. However, teens drawn to these supernatural teen television series might share similar characteristics or interests because they are all interested in the series for certain reasons. As cultural critic Kent A. Ono argues in his article, "To Be a Vampire on *Buffy the Vampire Slayer*: Race and ("Other") Socially Marginalizing Positions on Horror TV,"

> Like *Felicity, Dawson's Creek,* and *Sabrina the Teenage Witch, Buffy* has been praised for reaching out to teen female audiences, specifically. And, while the show's largest audience is in the 18 – 34 year-old range…media commentators regularly assume and discuss its specific appeal among teen girls.[149]

As Ono suggests, the larger audience of *Buffy the Vampire Slayer* undoubtedly includes both females and males outside of the teen audience, but there is a sizable teen female audience for this series. Likewise, both *Roswell* and *Joan of Arcadia* deal with topics and relationships that would appeal to teen girls. In addition, the similar storylines on all three series provide a common ground for the existence of these dramas in the supernatural teen television genre and normative world of teens.

The online message boards and reviews for each of these series tell us why the teen audience is drawn to these shows. In an online review, S. Mullen states that *Roswell* is "my favorite show ever, and I can't put my finger on exactly why. I can, however, put my finger on why I love it; great, relatable, well-acted characters, great episodes."[150] Similarly in an online review of *Joan of Arcadia*, one fan writes:

> This was one of the finest television series on the air. The writing was superb, the characters were believable, and the storylines were to die for. If you are still going through serious withdrawal since *Buffy the Vampire Slayer* and *Angel* went off the air, this show is for you. Granted, there are no vampires or monsters of the week – just your basic human demons – all our fears and foibles that we go through every day.[151]

---

149 Kent A. Ono, "To Be a Vampire on Buffy the Vampire Slayer: Race and ("Other") Socially Marginalizing Positions in Horror TV. *Fantasy Girls: Gender in the New Universe of Science Fiction and Fantasy Television*. Edited by Elyce Rae Helford. (Maryland: Roman & Littlefield Publishers, Inc, 2000), 165.

150 S. Mullen Amazon.com Review. March 25, 2006. *Roswell*, Season 1 Review.

151 J. Whitford Amazon.com review, March 15, 2005. *Joan of Arcadia*, Season 1.

The storylines, characters, and writing on all three series attracted viewers because they could relate to some aspect of the show. For many teens, the pressure of fitting into the normative high school lifestyle is a familiar situation, but not all adolescents were drawn to these series.

Several of the people who responded to the audience response surveys for this study were able to articulate their own opinions of why certain teens were drawn to these shows. One female in her late teens, who began watching *Roswell* when she was thirteen states,

> I guess if you look back on the show, it looks like the writers were trying to reach out to teens who didn't always fit in, or understand who they were, so that they could relate to the characters on the show. It was a more 'read between the lines' thing because on the surface, kids probably think that they can't relate to aliens? But between it all they realize that they have everyday problems just like themselves.[152]

Likewise, a male teen viewer of Buffy the Vampire Slayer contends,

> Throughout the run of BTVS there were messages that were intended to speak directly to teens. When a character has sex something bad happens; when they drink something bad happens; there were shows dealing with being an outcast, suicide, drugs, sexuality, peer pressure, race, fitting in, etc. Still the show never got too preachy with its messages. The writers were smart enough to work the messages in through the use of metaphors, allegories, and lots of vampires.[153]

These teen viewers of *Roswell* and *Buffy the Vampire Slayer* were able to recognize that the messages presented on each series were speaking to teens, whether directly or indirectly. The teen audience

---

152 Audience Response Survey received June 13, 2006. Respondent Information: Name: Jessica, Female, age 19.

153 Audience Response Survey received June 23, 2006. Respondent Information: Name: Anthony, Male, age 28.

of these shows were finding storylines and characters that they could connect with because of their own familiarity with such a situation or because of their desire to participate in something outside of the normative realm of teen culture. At the same time, one survey participant pointed out *Buffy* was not a regular teen television drama, but one that presented teens in a different way that has not been repeated in any other series. This teen female fan asserts:

> I think that the fact that this show ran seven seasons before it was canceled says a lot about teen television. It was so popular that even years afterward fans still gather for conventions, and buy merchandise. Teens then and now, want strong role models, we crave it. Now that I'm in my twenties I still am desperate for a show that gives a strong female role. Though I may occasionally watch TV nowadays, there isn't a show that I follow like I did *Buffy*. Reality doesn't excite me, why watch someone eat worms? It's debasing. I want to see the possibility of something new, something that I could only dream about happening to me.[154]

For this teen viewer, *Buffy* provided an outlet for wish fulfillment, a sense of finding one's place in the world outside of the everyday trials of teen life. Through these audience responses, it becomes clear that teen viewers were able to relate to the normative aspects of teen culture presented on these series, as well as seeing the potential to imagine their lives as something else – dreaming about possibilities of something new and something bigger than their normative existence.

The spiritual quests of Buffy, Liz, and Joan are the product of the adult constructions of adolescents as written in each of these teen drama series. The fact that both *Buffy the Vampire Slayer* and *Joan of Arcadia* focus on a female spiritual or supernatural warrior is indicative of a shift in the cultural approach to the significance of gender. For example, the female fighters on the television show *Charlie's Angels* of the 1970s were entirely dependent on their boss, Charlie, whose instructions came through Bosley. In sharp contrast

154 Audience Response Survey received July 8, 2006. Respondent Information: Name: Shannon, Female, age 27.

to these female characters are the female "chosen ones" seen on *Buffy*, *Roswell*, and *Joan of Arcadia*. Many of the teen fans of these shows appreciate the strong female characters on each series, as evidenced by the various responses received on this topic. One female fan of *Buffy* commented, "I think the characters were more complex than most TV show characters. I also liked that the girls were the strong ones saving the guys instead of the damsel in distress."[155] Similarly, one mother of a teen viewer of *Joan of Arcadia* posted the following on Amazon.com in 2005:

> For my teenage daughter, Joan has been a great character for her to watch. Joan is pretty but not skinny and empty-headed. She is a young lady who is thinking about the needs of others even though she also cares about her own needs. The stories really seem to capture what a teenager is like. It is hard to find wholesome teenage characters in shows these days. Teenage girls really need shows with characters like those in *Joan of Arcadia*.[156]

The female role models on each of these shows are able to take care of themselves and even perform supernatural tasks. The adult construction of adolescent reality in these characterizations displays a new sense of what it means to be a teen girl in America. No longer are females required to be the damsels in distress, and these television series present an alternative role for teen girls as strong females capable of surviving and standing on their own two feet. As one male viewer states:

> The typical arrangement in shows like these is scared little girl runs and screams and is either brutally killed or saved by the male hero. *Buffy* turns the table on this stereotype and shows the petite little girl as the hero. Normally the males are the stronger of the two sexes. While on *Buffy* of the four main characters (Buffy, Willow, Xander, and Giles) the female characters are the ones with the power.[157]

155 Audience Response Survey received July 8, 2006. Respondent Information: Name: Shannon, Female, age 27.

156 Deborah L. Riva Amazon.com review, July 16, 2005. *Joan of Arcadia*, Season 1.

157 Audience Response Survey received June 23, 2006. Respondent Information: Name: Anthony, Male, age 28.

On *Buffy*, as on *Joan of Arcadia* and *Roswell*, the main female characters are strong and in pursuit of their own identity and spiritual quests as discussed earlier in this study. They do not need a man to protect them, and these teen girls are warriors in every sense of the word – they not only look after themselves, they are also saving the world.

The adult writers of each of these television series are writing for a specific audience, one that includes a large number of teens. Instead of incorrectly assuming things about teen culture, the adults seem to get many things right in their portrayal of normative teen culture. According to one teen viewer of *Buffy*, the writers were speaking to the teen audience. "I think the writers were trying to give teens a moral basis to decide on how to react to these types of things happening in real life."[158] The normative teen problems of identity crisis, sexual experimentation, peer pressure, and romance were incorporated into the messages written into the script of these series. Many of the audience responses for *Joan of Arcadia, Roswell,* and *Buffy the Vampire Slayer* go on to suggest that teenagers are presented accurately. One female teen viewer of *Joan of Arcadia* argues, "The teenagers on the show seemed realistic and relatable to me. Every one of them represented a typical teenager you would find at any school."[159] This idea of stereotypical teens being represented on the series is repeated by a viewer of *Buffy the Vampire Slayer* who claims:

> I think that the show did a good job in portraying teenagers. Again, all demonic activity aside, they were still self-involved, sometimes vain, sometimes shallow, often over-emotional, and usually quite silly. There was a broad spectrum represented (personality wise at least), we had smart teen (Willow), not so smart but very funny teen (Xander), popular teen (Cordelia), and even the bad teen (Faith).[160]

---

158 Audience Response Survey receivedJune 29, 2006. Respondent Information: Name: Danielle, Female, age 21.

159 Audience Response Survey received September 29, 2006. Respondent Information: Name: Sarah, Female, age 22.

160 Audience Response Survey receivedJune 13, 2006. Repondent Information: Name: Kimberly, Female, age 26

These teen stereotypes can be observed on high school campuses across the country, as pointed out by Pamela Perry's ethnographic research at two high schools in California at the turn of the 21st century. Perry examines this idea of normal or stereotypical teen culture as she looks at the racial identities of teens at Clavey High and Valley Groves High. Perry asserts,

> Although each group on campus formed part of a diverse mosaic and had unique, identifying characteristics, a norm-other logic was the overarching principle by which students organized and made sense of their social world. The "normal" and popular students were, basically, those in compliance with school and adult mainstream expectations, and the "other" kids posed some contradiction to that.[161]

Thus, the normative aspects of teen culture include the stereotypical teen characters seen on *Buffy the Vampire Slayer, Roswell,* and *Joan of Arcadia* as well as on high school campuses across the nation. These characters are identifiable to the teen audience, because they have encountered the popular teen, the smart teen, and the rebellious teen in their own lives. Even within the subculture of teens, there are distinct groups of teens that are often called cliques. One look at a high school campus, the locus of teen culture in modern-day America, gives any observer a glimpse into the complex group associations that exist within teen culture. As Thomas Hine states:

> The typical suburban high school is occupied by groups of teens who express themselves through music, dress, tattoos and piercing, obsessive hobbies, consumption patterns, extracurricular activities,m drug habits and sex practices. These tribes hang out in different parts of the school, go to different parts of town. Once it was possible to speak of a youth culture, but now there is a range of youth subcultures, and clans, coteries, and cliques within those.[162]

161 Pamela Perry, *Shades of White: White Kids and Racial Identities in High School* (North Carolina: Duke University Press, 2002), 30.

162 Audience Response Surveyy received June 13, 2006. Respondent Information: Name Kimberly, Female, age 26.

Throughout Hine's text, it is clear that he sees the American high school as the center of activity for teenagers. The indicators of participation in this teen culture are seen in clothing, music, and other popular culture interests, hobbies and ties to consumer culture.

The real teen viewers of *Buffy* were able to articulate their own perception of high school normalcy as presented in this television series. One female viewer stated, "I found the teens to be pretty relatable, except for the slayer aspect. But all the stereotypes were present: The Brain, the Nerd, The Outcast, the Cheerleader. As time went by, the stereotypes were stripped down to show the real human aspect of these characters."[163]

Likewise, another teen viewer points out that she was able to recognize the typical high school characters on *Buffy* that she had encountered in her own life. "Though rather campy and shallow, teens on the show were pretty realistic. Stereotypes such as band geeks, computer nerds, the popular crowd, cheerleaders are all pretty relatable to my high school experience."[164] The voices of these real teen viewers of *Buffy the Vampire Slayer* highlight the stereotypical nature of these characters, but they also provide evidence of the realistic portrayal of teens on the show. The fact that these real teens are able to relate to the fictive teens because of their own experiences in teen culture suggests that the characterization of teens on these selected supernatural teen television dramas are in many ways representative of real life for many teens.

The supernatural and spiritual elements are another aspect of these three teen drama series that sets them apart and allows them to speak to real teens in new ways than other teen television shows. This is definitely the most obvious difference between *Buffy* and *Veronica Mars* or *Roswell* and *Dawson's Creek*. Instead of acting as an

163 Audience Response Survey received June 13, 2006. Repondent Information: Name: Kimberly, Female, age 26.

164 Audience Response Survey distributed at CSUF in Fall 2006 American Studies undergraduate courses. Respondent Information: Name: Jennifer, Female, age 23.

assistant to her former-Sheriff turned private investigator father as Veronica Mars did on her series, Buffy Summers is busy fighting assassins and demons in her Homecoming gown.[165] *Veronica Mars* is a television show that ran for three seasons on the CW network, which is the network that bought out (the WB) on which *Buffy the Vampire Slayer* originally aired. *Veronica Mars* aired from 2004 to 2007, and featured a sassy lead female character who lives in the private investigator world alongside her father as they search to uncover the mystery of who murdered her best friend. While not supernatural, Veronica does have some similar qualities to Buffy. However, the confrontation with the supernatural and spiritual worlds combined with the normative high school elements set the teen characters of *Joan of Arcadia, Roswell,* and *Buffy the Vampire Slayer* apart from other teen television dramas on air at this unique time in American society.

In considering the spiritual and supernatural roles of the main characters of these three teen series, it is crucial to look at the ways in which these roles influence the unique status of fictive teens on television as well as real teens. Do these supernatural and spiritual circumstances take away from the role of teens such as Buffy, Liz, and Joan in teen culture? The answer, I believe, is a resounding "No." Instead, these supernatural and spiritual qualities that the chosen teen characters on television possess are additive characteristics. One female viewer of *Buffy* agrees that the supernatural elements are helpful in building a strong central character. This viewer maintains, "She had everyday teenage dramas…but then the supernatural was in a way a release from her teenage drama and she stopped the evil element from winning."[166] One teen fan of *Roswell* agrees that the supernatural elements in this teen television drama add to the search for identity experienced by teens – both fictive and real teens. She argues, "I think their powers made it more interesting, and fun for the eyes. It went along with the alien theme, and helped develop the idea of them discovering just who

---

165 *Buffy the Vampire Slayer*, Season 3, Episode 5.

166 Audience Response Survey received June 13, 2006. Respondent Information: Name: Kimberly, Female, age 26.

they were."[167] The supernatural elements display how special and set apart teens are, not only the fictive teen characters of television dramas but also the real teens who are watching these teen series. As cultural critic Patricia Hersch comments:

> America's own adolescents have become strangers. They are a tribe apart, remote, mysterious, vaguely threatening. The tribal notion is so commonplace that it is hard to know whether it derives from the kids or from adults, but the result is that somewhere in the transition from twelve to thirteen, our nation's children slip into a netherworld of adolescence that too often becomes a self-fulfilling prophecy of estrangement.[168]

This tribe of teens has been left feeling lost in American culture, and the wish fulfillment that is offered by teen television dramas such as *Buffy*, *Joan of Arcadia*, and *Roswell* gives real teens a chance to see their lives in a new way. Instead of feeling ostracized from dominant culture and lost in the shuffle of fast-paced, consumer-culture-driven American life, teens are given an outlet to believe their lives can have an impact beyond their own existence, just as the main characters on these television series have been called to do something spiritually or supernaturally significant with their lives. As one female teen fan states in the audience response surveys for *Roswell*, "What teenager doesn't wish they had some extraordinary power that made them truly unique? That is what the ultimate dream of any teenager is, right?"[169]

The teens on *Buffy*, *Roswell*, and *Joan of Arcadia* are exceptional because of their links to the spiritual and supernatural worlds. Are all teens as unique as these teen characters? How do teens fit as members of a subculture within the dominant American culture? The outsider status of the teen characters on these television series

---

167 Audience Response Survey received June 13, 2006. Respondent Information: Name: Jessica, Female, age 19.

168 Hersch, 14.

169 Audience Response survey distributed in American Studies undergraduate classes in Fall 2006 at CSU Fullerton. Respondent Information: Name: Blair, Female, age 24.

are a result of each teen playing dual roles – one as a participant of teen culture and the other as a member of dominant culture. One major issue that is brought to light through these shows is the question of how to exist in this dual-role world. This question has a huge cultural impact because it not only examines the complicated life of adolescents, it also requires involvement from participants of dominant culture – namely adults. As a member of this adult dominant culture, Patricia Hersch argues in her conclusion to *A Tribe Apart*, "We have to reconnect the adolescent community to ours. It is not so hard. We just need to reach out and embrace them and take the time to get to know them – one by one, as individuals, not a tribe."[170] As Hersch contends, it is crucial to look at teens as individual people, not as one group whose members are completely identical to each other. Although teens do comprise a distinct subculture, they cannot all be classified as one particular type of person. Teens in America must be considered as individuals as well as members of teen culture.

In looking at teens as members of a unique subculture set apart from dominant culture, one must give attention to the indicators of belonging to this specific subculture of teens. The cultural markers of distinction for teens include language, symbols of popularity, specific characteristics of teen friendships and romantic relationships, and the artifacts of consumerism as seen in clothing, accessories, and other consumer products. In discussing the characters on *Buffy*, one male fan of the series states, "The character development on other shows seemed to be very shallow compared to those on *Buffy*. The characters also had a unique way of speaking [and their speech was] often littered with hidden meaning of pop culture references that many people missed."[171] As discussed in previous chapters, the product placement and pop culture references on shows such as *Roswell, Buffy the Vampire Slayer,* and *Joan of Arcadia* are clear indicators of the influence of consumer culture on the surreal teen characters in these television dramas. Also, the language of teenagers is an indicator of their membership in this distinct subculture. Yet, it is crucial to recognize that all teens are not carbon-copies of one

170 Hersch, 372.

171 Audience Response Survey received June 23, 2006. Respondent Information: Name: Anthony, Male, age 28.

another, but are individuals who share common characteristics with other members of the teen culture.

From the very first episode of *Buffy the Vampire Slayer*, Buffy Summers is presented as a teen girl with interest in her appearance and how her clothing, hair, and makeup mark her as a specific type of participant in teen culture. In this first episode, Buffy is approached by Cordelia and quizzed on various aspects of popular culture and what is considered cool among teens at the time.

> Cordelia: Of course, we do have to test your coolness factor. You're from L.A., so you can skip the written, but let's see. Vamp nail polish?
> Buffy: Um, over?
> Cordelia: So over. James Spader?
> Buffy: He needs to call me.
> Cordelia: Frappuccino's?
> Buffy: Trendy, but tasty.
> Cordelia: John Tesh.
> Buffy: The Devil.
> Cordelia: That was pretty much a gimme, but you passed.
> Buffy: Oh, good.[172]

One can hardly imagine such a conversation taking place among adults, but this represents a common exchange among teenagers in the late 20th century. Buffy's knowledge of the acceptable interests of a certain clique of teenagers grants her membership in this specific group. Here, both an awareness of certain aspects of consumer culture and language are indicators of the involvement of Buffy and Cordelia in teen culture. Again, real teen viewers are able to identify this relationship of the fictive teen characters to the links between consumer culture and real teen experiences. A male fan recognizes the use of popular culture references in *Buffy the Vampire Slayer*. He says:

> *Buffy* had the ability to entertain all different types of people. The writing was smart and layered so that it catered to the intellectuals; it had action and gore for those that could care less about the psychology; it had drama and continuity

172 *Buffy the Vampire Slayer*, Season 1, Episode 1.

> dealing with love and loss, life and death; it had comedy and tons of pop culture references, etc., etc.…I can't think of another show, particularly one geared towards teens that has accomplished so much.[173]

For this teen viewer, the pop culture references are just one of the elements that set this series apart. The fact that he acknowledges the use of consumerism on this television series and the familiarity that teens have with popular culture is indicative of the impact of pop culture references and product placement for real teen viewers. Also, the fact that this was the only participant in the audience response surveys who realized that the pop culture references did have an impact on teen viewers suggests that many of these viewers merely accept the many aspects of consumerism woven into the storylines, dialogue, and setting of these television series as normative pieces of teen culture.

Language is often a symbol of teen culture. For instance, on *Joan of Arcadia*, Adam is usually blunt and to the point, as seen in the "State of Grace" episode from season one. Joan asks Adam for his opinion on something, and Adam responds, "I usually don't listen to what's going on unless I hear my name."[174] Although many adults might think these same thoughts, to express them verbally is something that is much more likely to happen within teen culture than mainstream adult culture.

The specific nature of language among teens is further evidence of language as a subcultural symbol among teens. The superficial conversation between Buffy and Cordelia in the first episode of the series proves to Cordelia that Buffy is worthy of Cordelia's time and attention. The language here also acts as a marker of Buffy and Cordelia's participation in teen culture, as they glibly reference popular culture figures such as James Spader and John Tesh, as well as consumer items such as nail polish and Frappuccino's. Likewise on *Roswell*, the teens are often discussing issues such as sex, love,

173 Audience Response Survey received June 23, 2006. Respondent Information: Name: Anthony, Male, age 28.

174 *Joan of Arcadia*, Season 1, Episode 14.

parents, and school straightforwardly. Again, one real teen viewer points out this realistic portrayal of teens in her audience response survey. She relates, "Teenagers are presented as normal teens that deal with love, relationships, fighting, sex, etc..... the only difference is these teens are aliens or are friends with aliens."[175] The dialogue between Maria and Liz in episode two of season one regarding the eraser room is just one example of the direct language used by teens, especially in their conversations with one another. Maria says to Liz, "The eraser room does two things. Cleans erasers, and takes our innocence. Do you know what I mean, by 'takes our innocence' Liz? The eraser room has taken some of the best of us."[176] This pointed language is another example of the normative qualities of teen culture that are presented on these television series.

The specific characteristics that are often common among teen friendships and romances are also signs of the subculture of teens. As discussed earlier, the female best friendships that are seen between Buffy and Willow, Joan and Grace, and Liz and Maria are typical of many teen girls. Also, the teen romances of each of the main characters are similar in many ways. The love between Angel and Buffy, and also between Max and Liz is presented as a powerful and passionate attraction to one another, but also a deep emotional connection between the characters. Many times on *Roswell*, Liz attempts to express these feelings verbally. Even Tess, the girl who tries to come between Liz and Max, admits that she always knew there was a connection between them that she could not break. Tess says to Liz in "Four Aliens and a Baby" episode of season three, "Max loves you. Every time we were together, every time we kissed he was thinking of you. He had these flashes that I saw and they were always of you."[177] Despite the supernatural elements of their connection, Max and Liz's romance is quite typical of many first love experiences of teens. For this reason, it is easily identified by many of the real teen viewers as the most prominent relationship on *Roswell*. One viewer responds that the most significant relationship is

175 Audience Response Survey received September 29, 2006. Respondent Information: Sarah, Female, age 22.

176 *Roswell*, Season 1, Episode 2.

177 *Roswell*, Season 3, Episode 17.

between "Max and Liz because they were the 'modern day' Romeo and Juliet. Always a story of them and their love. Even when they weren't together, that was a storyline."[178] This romance is one that many real teens are able to relate to because the emotions, passion, and constant dramatic tension between Liz and Max is familiar to real life experience of teens.

Similarly, the intensity, desire, and all-consuming nature of many teen romances is also seen in the love shared by Buffy and Angel. Again, their supernatural experiences as the slayer and a tortured-with-a-soul vampire complicate their relationship on a different level than the romances of other teens. "Most of Buffy's decisions were based on her relationship with Angel," one female viewer argues. "It was the way the writers brought up a lot of the issues aimed at teens, such as dealing with love, relationships that others don't approve of, and the consequences of sex."[179] Another female fan of *Buffy* agrees that Buffy and Angel's relationship was the most significant of the series. She says:

> The relationship showed that no matter the supernatural powers or human desire you possess or how desperately you want to make a relationship work sometimes you just have to let go. Although you may love someone beyond reason, the most mature thing you can do is to walk away because you love that person enough to let them go. This goes along with the storyline in season three about growing up and realizing that what you so badly want, sometimes you just have to realize is not destined to be yours.[180]

Many real teens have been confronted with feelings that feel much too big for them, and this undeniable pull to be with someone

---

178 Audience Response Survey distributed in American Studies undergraduate classes at CSU Fullerton in Fall 2006. Respondent Information: Name: Blair, Female, age 24.

179 Audience Response Survey received July 8, 2006. Respondent Information: Name: Shannon, Female, age 27.

180 Audience Response Survey receivedJune 13, 2006. Respondent Information: Name: Kimberly, Female, age 26.

who is not necessarily good for you. Those real teens can relate to Buffy and Angel in this way.

Oftentimes in teen romances, the significant other becomes the central person in a teen's life, as everyone else seems to be less important because of the overwhelming need to spend every waking moment with this person. This feeling, which can be accurately described more as infatuation than anything else, often clouds Buffy's judgment when it comes to Angel. In the tenth episode of season two, Buffy states, "You can attack me, you can send assassins after me, that's fine. But nobody messes with my boyfriend."[181] Buffy and Angel's relationship, much like Liz's relationship with Max and Joan's relationship with Adam, is an indicator of their involvement in the subculture of teens. The overly dramatized feelings, fights, and passion for one another is heightened in this liminal stage of life when every situation appears to be more life-altering than the reality of it.

Family relationships are extremely important on all three series, but in different ways. On *Joan of Arcadia*, the presence of family is significant, while on *Roswell* and *Buffy*, the absence of parents and family support is important to the development of the main teen characters. Changing family dynamics affect many teens across the country, as recent data suggests that half of all American children will witness their parents' divorce before they turn 18.[182] Real teens deal with various family problems on a daily basis from divorce to abandonment to a lack of interaction with parents and siblings. Perhaps the most striking relationship for all three teen series under analysis here is the father/daughter relationship. Buffy, Joan, and Liz all have relationships with their mothers, but the father/daughter relationship dynamic is sorely lacking on *Buffy* and severely strained on *Roswell* because of Liz's relationship with Max. Only Joan appears to have a solid relationship with her father. Sara Shandler discusses the need for a positive father/daughter dynamic during the teen years in *Ophelia Speaks*. She writes,

---

181 *Buffy the Vampire Slayer*, Season 2, Episode 10.

182 Shaheen & Gordon, Attorneys at Law. https://www.shaheengordon.com/blog/2024/january/understanding-the-impact-of-divorce-on-children/. Accessed December 1, 2025.

> I hope hearing the voices of girls who ask for nothing more than their father's caring attention will break through the isolation suffered by girls with similar longing. I also expect these stories will engender an appreciation for fathers who do their best to maintain a connection with us as we deal with the demands of adolescence.[183]

One real teen viewer of *Joan of Arcadia* recognized the relationship between Joan and her father as the most significant on the series. When asked what the most prominent relationship on this series was, this viewer responded, "Joan's relationship with her father, who is a cop. This is the most important relationship because it shows that she is 'Daddy's little girl.'"[184] The fact that Joan is seen by this viewer as "Daddy's little girl" suggests that Joan's relationship with her father is one that reinforces positive self-esteem and confidence in who she is as an individual. This observation goes hand-in-hand with Shandler's argument that the father/daughter relationship during a female's teen years is extremely significant to the development of that individual's self-esteem.

The lack of parental involvement on both *Buffy* and *Roswell* is clearly in opposition to the many interactions between family members on *Joan of Arcadia*. One teen viewer of Joan points out, "Overall, the relationships between the family members and Joan's relationship with God were key."[185] On the other hand, a female teen viewer of *Roswell* points out that although the teen characters were realistically portrayed, the family dynamics were not as convincing. She argues, "The whole nature of the show wasn't very realistic – but the relationships were. I thought that it showed what a good friendship was. Also, it seemed to ignore parental control (for the most part) which wasn't all that realistic."[186] So, for many teen

183 Shandler, 78.

184 Audience Response Survey distributed in American Studies undergraduate classes at CSU Fullerton in Fall 2006. Respondent Information: Name: Jonathan, Male, age 24.

185 Audience Response Survey received September 29, 2006. Respondent Information: Sarah, Female, age 22.

186 Audience Response Survey distributed in American Studies undergraduate classes at CSU Fullerton in Fall 2006. Respondent Information: Name: Blair,

viewers the absence of parents is not a realistic representation of teen culture. Instead, the involvement of parents in their lives, however limited or complicated because of changes to the family over the past several decades, is a very real aspect of normative teen life.

Moving away from the relationships of teen characters with their family, it is crucial to examine the link between the spiritual and identity quests of characters such as Buffy, Liz, and Joan. The idea that these teen characters serve a purpose both in teen culture and in the supernatural realm in which they each exist is an ongoing theme in all three shows, and one that is discussed by the real teen participants of my audience response surveys. As one *Buffy* viewer articulates, "Aside from the relationships with Buffy's friends and love interests, I think the most prominent relationship would be with herself. Every season Buffy struggled between her life as a slayer and herself as a teenager. Her life as the slayer got in the way of her love life and her friendships."[187] The complications that Buffy faced as a result of her existence in two worlds – the world of teens and the world of vampires – made her involvement in normative teen culture much more difficult as she attempted to keep her supernatural identity secret.

Buffy the Vampire Slayer, Roswell, and *Joan of Arcadia* allow the teen audience to imagine themselves as more than average teens. The teen audience of these shows can conceive of ways in which they might impact the world. Prior to the events of September 11, 2001, which was followed by a culture of fear in American society (not unlike the more recent post-COVID pandemic response in 2020), the popularity of supernatural teen television dramas was the result of the possibility within American culture to have more than one answer to the large spiritual questions that many individuals face in their lifetime. As Lynn Schofield Clark discusses in her analysis of religion and the media in American culture, "The increasingly multicultural and religiously plural environment in which today's

Female, age 24.

187 Audience Response Survey distributed in American Studies undergraduate classes at CSU Fullerton in Fall 2006. Respondent Information: Name: Valerie, Female, age 22.

teens' lives influence their approach to religion and contributes to this openness of possibilities."[188] Clark goes on to explain how the religious and racial differences within the United States encourages young people to explore the idea that there are many options for religion and spiritual beliefs. One female teen viewer of *Joan of Arcadia* expresses her own opinion of the reception of spiritual shows on television. She contends that television series that have an emphasis on God or the spiritual world of angels usually did not last long on the airwaves in the early 21st century. This viewer asserts, "I think that people are so set in their ways that they don't want to be reminded about religion, or God, or angels. Or about their faults and what they need to change."[189] The subject of faith and the unknown world of supernatural and spiritual beings is oftentimes frightening for individuals who are not accustomed to thinking about such subjects. The fact that *Buffy*, *Roswell*, and *Joan of Arcadia* all touch on the spiritual or supernatural realm suggests to teen viewers that there is a whole different world out there beyond the normative teen culture, and this idea could be appealing to teens who are not exactly popular or accepted by their peers.

The willingness to accept more than one religious viewpoint as valid unlocks the door for limitless potential in the realm of identity for teens. The question of identity for adolescents in America is often highlighted by the characters on *Buffy*, *Roswell*, and *Joan*. In *All Grown Up and No Place to Go: Teenagers in Crisis*, Elkind argues, "More than anything else, the attainment of a healthy sense of identity and a feeling of self-esteem gives young people a perspective, a way of looking at themselves and others…"[190] As Elkind discusses throughout his work, teenagers today are in crisis because they have no role to play in society. He argues that they are no longer children, but are also not yet adults. This is the liminal quality of the teen years as a life stage, in that teens are no longer children but are not

188 Clark, 228.

189 Audience Response Survey received July 11, 2006. Respondent Information: Kayla, Female, age 15.

190 Elkind, *All Grown Up and No Place to Go: Teenagers in Crisis Revised Edition.* (Massachusetts: Da Capo Press, 1998), 196.

mature enough to be treated as adults. They are literally between life stages, and the crisis occurs because society has not defined the roles to solidify the cultural importance of this stage. Again, the real teen viewers recognize the dual nature of roles played by the teen characters on these three shows. One female *Buffy* fan says, "In almost all the seasons, Buffy tries to balance what she calls 'normal life' and slaying."[191] Another *Buffy* fan suggests that the supernatural elements simply add to the complications of life as a teenager. He maintains, "The supernatural just adds another facet to the problems/challenges the characters would already have to face."[192] Therefore, for the teen characters on these television series, they are not only faced with the identity crisis brought on by normative teen culture that Elkind discusses, but they are also faced with supernatural elements that complicate their identity quest even more.

The themes of friendship, romance, family discord, and identity are all dominant throughout *Buffy, Roswell,* and *Joan of Arcadia.* Not only are these the themes that have been picked out throughout this study as the dynamic between normative teen culture and the supernatural world of these fictive teens is explored, but they are also the same themes that are recognized as important and influential by real teen viewers. The dual roles of the central female characters – Liz, Joan, and Buffy – are the shaping force of each of these television series. As cultural critic Kent Ono discusses in his article on *Buffy the Vampire Slayer*, Buffy is constantly balancing her roles as a teen girl and as the vampire slayer. Ono writes,

> At home, we see Buffy sleeping in her bed, often dreaming about monsters, talking with her mother downstairs in the kitchen, chatting on the phone with Willow, getting slaying supplies from her closet and putting them in her bag, or especially in earlier episodes, before her mother knows she is the slayer, climbing in and out of her window at night or when grounded.[193]

---

191 Audience Response Survey received June 29, 2006. Respondent Information: Danielle, Female, age 21.

192 Audience Response Survey received August 1, 2006. Respondent Information: Ernie, Male, age 24.

193 Ono, 171.

This combination of normative (dreaming, talking to her mother) and supernatural (dreams of monsters, gathering slayer supplies) creates a complicated identity crisis for Buffy that participants in normative teen culture do not have to confront. However, teens can identify with Buffy because they too participate in two worlds – the dominant culture and subculture of teens.

Likewise, Liz and Joan must cope with their supernatural callings while attending school dances, working part-time jobs, and talking with their parents. At the same time, Liz, Joan and Buffy also experience many of the same feelings and situations that are considered to be a part of normal teen life. For example, the romantic relationships between the central female characters and their boyfriends were easily identifiable by the real teen viewers as typical teen romances (with the demon-slaying, alien-hunting, and conversations with God aside). Also, the family relationships (or lack thereof) on each of these shows were topics that spoke directly to the real teen viewers. For one viewer, *Roswell* "shows that teen television can be used to help teens relate to others, and not feel so alone in their crazy, confusing teenage years."[194] Another viewer of *Roswell* argues that "supernatural powers make the main characters more human, because of the way they use their powers to save lives."[195] These real teen voices suggest that these television series are, in many ways, representative of normative teen culture and relationships that many teens encounter during these formative years.

The real teen respondents of audience response surveys distributed in undergraduate university classes and among viewers of these teen drama series expressed their opinions on the portrayal of teens on these shows. One female viewer of *Buffy* writes: "Teenagers were represented on the show as having thoughts and opinions that mattered and whose actions had consequences and

---

194 Audience Response Survey received June 13, 2006. Respondent Information: Jessica, Female, age 19.

195 Audience Response Survey distributed in American Studies undergraduate classes at CSU Fullerton in Fall 2006. Respondent Information: Name: Jonathan, Male, age 24.

whose mistakes were learned from."[196] At the same time, the relationships that teens have with their friends and family also carried messages that spoke loud and clear to another *Buffy* fan. She points out, "It was said on the show that Buffy survived longer than any other slayer because she maintained friendships and had the bond of family. I think that this message was one of the most important from the entire show."[197] Consequently, the combination of the normative pressures of teen culture coupled with the demands placed on Buffy, Liz, and Joan by their supernatural roles truly set these teen characters apart from other fictive teens on television. The character of Buffy gave teen audiences hope that they too would be able to play a larger role in society, and have an impact on the lives of others. She allows the audience to imagine their lives as something bigger. Because of the shift to home-based activities such as watching television in the last half of the 20th century, the role of the teen audience at the turn of the 21st century when *Buffy* was airing, became a multimedia experience. Not only are the teens watching the television series, they are going online and discussing the shows with their peers in chat rooms and message boards. This network of technology that emerged at the turn of the 21st century continues into the 2020s and has exploded even more with the popularity of social media platforms like Snapchat, Instagram, Facebook and TikTok. The audience has become the star of the show in many respects.

196 Audience Response Survey received June 26, 2006. Respondent Information: Kimberly, Female, age 26.

197 Audience Response Survey received June 29, 2006. Respondent Information: Danielle, Female, age 21.

Coming of Age

Chapter 10

Adolescents as the Real and Imagined "Chosen Ones"

Adolescents are often represented as the chosen ones, both in reality and in teen television dramas of the 1990s and early 2000s. The liminal stage of adolescence, the element of mystery that often surrounds the American teenager in their unpredictable thought and behavior patterns, and the treatment of adolescents as a distinct subgroup in the youth culture of America all factor in to the representation of teens as chosen ones in our culture. Yet, teenagers can also be seen as outsiders, troubled individuals who stand in opposition to the dominant order of things. This precarious position held by adolescents in American culture is one that defines who they are and how they react to the adults that they must interact with on a regular basis.

One of the greatest messages of *Buffy the Vampire Slayer*, one that still stands the test of time over twenty years later, is that in being the chosen one of her generation, the ultimate choice Buffy makes at the end of the series is to decide that she should not be the only chosen one. She extends that power to all females with the potential to be chosen, to be called as the vampire slayer. Buffy re-writes the narrative. She empowers an entire generation of females to fight on the side of good. This message of female empowerment is not seen in the same magnitude in any other shows on the air at this time, especially not ones with a targeted teen audience like shows on the WB of the 1990s and early 2000s.

In the post-September 11th culture in America after the terrorist attacks in 2001, the constant possibility of an attack and the questions of identity and inquiries about other life forms or threats to national security surrounded us. Now, over twenty years later and on the heels of a global pandemic, we don't just worry about physical attacks, but about viruses and our health, and about cyber security, identity fraud and hackers attacking us using technology. Teenagers also still pose a threat to dominant society in that they question the order of things – they are a societal "other" that proposes alternatives for a different kind of future. They're capable of re-writing the narrative once again, and that scares people in positions of power.

Teens have the power to change things – and most of the time, they do not even realize their collective power. In certain instances, we see a glimpse of the power of teens to make a difference. For instance, when school shootings occurred in the late 1990s and teens rallied in support of their fallen friends and teachers, America saw the impact of teens on our culture at large. In small gatherings on university and high school campuses across the country, we see examples of teens raising funds for charity, speaking out for activism, and rallying for reproductive rights for women. It is in these times that the power of teens to make a difference is truly seen.

Unfortunately, by largely eliminating the supernatural from teen television dramas in the early 2000s, we have essentially tried to squelch the questioning and questing of American teens. Teens have found a new way to embark on identity and spiritual quests, and can now share that journey for all of their friends and fans to see online. Shows like *Buffy the Vampire Slayer*, *Roswell*, and *Joan of Arcadia* resisted the dominant cultural ideology in their search for a teen identity and a calling for these adolescents who are struggling to find their way in a world created for them by others. Only when the true voice of real teens is heard in the way that characters like Buffy Summers, Liz Parker and Joan Girardi have spoken out and re-wrote the narrative, will the power of teens truly be felt in American culture. The impact that teenagers could have in modern society once they collectively speak their minds and carve out a distinct place for themselves in American culture could potentially change the world. Their collective efforts will be capable of shifting the paradigm of thought and the ways in which we define this unique stage of life. Social media has given birth to new authentic voices, so only time will tell how loud those declarations become, and how much change is truly possible.

About the author

Jenn Burton is a professor of American Studies at California State University, Fullerton and a lifelong student of all things culture studies related. Her undergraduate and graduate programs in American Studies at CSU Fullerton have come full circle as she now teaches the subjects she was so passionate about learning as a student two decades ago. Living a purposeful life and being authentically herself has not come easy, but it is a dream come true.

Jenn is also a mom of four and an avid reader. If she's not working or spending time at home with a good book or her family, you can find her cheering on her youngest kids on the soccer field or basketball court. In rare sightings without a book, laptop or her kids, you might find her enjoying a quiet meal with her husband, Nicholas, whom she credits with being her best friend and source of grounding in this crazy, beautiful life.

www.ingramcontent.com/pod-product-compliance
Ingram Content Group UK Ltd.
Pitfield, Milton Keynes, MK11 3LW, UK
UKHW062258290726
14090UKWH00017B/767

9 781960 596895